CHURCHILL: SHORTS
Short Plays By
Caryl Churchill

LOVESICK

ABORTIVE

NOT NOT NOT NOT NOT
ENOUGH OXYGEN

SCHREBER'S NERVOUS ILLNESS

THE HOSPITAL AT THE
TIME OF THE REVOLUTION

THE JUDGE'S WIFE

THE AFTER-DINNER JOKE

SEAGULLS

THREE MORE SLEEPLESS NIGHTS

HOT FUDGE

NICK HERN BOOKS
London

A Nick Hern Book

Churchill: Shorts first published in 1990 as an original
paperback by Nick Hern Books.
Reprinted 1993 by Nick Hern Books Limited,
14 Larden Road, London W3 7ST

Set in Baskerville by 🅐 Tek Art Ltd

Printed and bound in Great Britain
by Cox & Wyman, Reading, Berks

British Library Cataloguing in Publication Data
  Churchill, Caryl
  Churchill Shorts
  I. Title
  822.914
  ISBN: 1 85459 085 5

Contents

Introduction

Caryl Churchill

A Chronology of Performed Plays

PLAY	PERFORMED
	(s=stage,
	r=radio,
	t=television)
Downstairs	1958*s*
You've No Need to be Frightened	1961*r*
Having a Wonderful Time	1960*s*
Easy Death	1961*s*
The Ants	1962*r*
Lovesick	1966*r*
Identical Twins	1968*r*
Abortive	1971*r*
Not Not Not Not Not Enough Oxygen	1971*r*
Schreber's Nervous Illness	1972*r*
Henry's Past	1972*r*
The Judge's Wife	1972*t*
Owners	1972*s*
Moving Clocks Go Slow	1975*s*
Turkish Delight	1974*t*
Perfect Happiness	1973*r*
Objections to Sex and Violence	1975*s*
Traps	1977*s*
Vinegar Tom	1976*s*
Light Shining in Buckinghamshire	1976*s*
Floorshow (contributor to)	1977*s*
The After-Dinner Joke	1978*t*
The Legion Hall Bombing	1979*t*
Softcops	1983*s*
Cloud Nine	1979*s*
Three More Sleepless Nights	1980*s*
Crimes	1981*t*
Top Girls	1982*s*
Fen	1983*s*

Introduction

The first of these plays was written in 1965, the last in 1989.
The first four are radio plays that could possibly be done in
the theatre. *Lovesick* and *Schreber* have that movement
between being inside someone's head and out among
extraordinary events that works particularly well on radio,
though *Schreber* was also done as a one-man show by Kenneth
Haigh at the Soho Poly. *Abortive* and *Not . . . Enough Oxygen*,
both with one set and few characters, could easily be staged.
It's slightly unnerving to read *Not . . . Oxygen* twenty years
later. It's more obviously relevant now than it was then.

Hospital and *Seagulls* are two stage plays that were never
done. *Hospital* was written around the same time as *Schreber*,
and combined my interest in Fanon and in Laing; Algeria
had interested me since the fifties. Fanon's *Black Faces, White
Masks* was one of the things (along with Genet) that led to
Joshua, the black servant, being played by a white in *Cloud
Nine*. *Seagulls* was written in 1978 and felt too much as if it
was about not being able to write for me to want it done at
the time. I promptly wrote *Softcops* and *Cloud Nine* and forgot
about it.

The Judge's Wife was written for TV in the early seventies
and feels to me like a TV play, depending very much for its
effect on the filmed flashbacks. It was a play I wrote first and
looked for a slot for afterwards, whereas *The After-Dinner Joke*
(1977) was written because Margaret Matheson wanted to
produce a series of Plays for Today for the BBC on public
issues and suggested I look at charities. I admired two
extremes on TV, extreme naturalism and extreme non-
naturalism – (Loach, Joffe; Monty Python). I went for the
second – no of course it's not as funny as Monty Python. It's
stageable I think if anyone would enjoy trying with a small
group doubling and quintupling. Some references would
need updating but the basic issue seems to be the same now.

When I wrote *Sleepless Nights* (1979) for Les Waters, who
directed it at the Soho Poly, I wanted two kinds of quarrel –
the one where you can't speak and the one where you both
talk at once. When I was writing *Top Girls* I first wrote a
draft of the dinner scene with one speech after another and
then realised it would be better if the talk overlapped in a
similar way. Having got a taste for it I've gone on
overlapping in most things I've written since.

I wrote *Hot Fudge* ten years later. Max Stafford-Clark, who was about to direct *Icecream* was concerned at it being so short, and suggested I write something to go with it. I made it so the two actors who doubled in *Icecream* could play the main parts in *Hot Fudge* and the other four double as their friends. In the end I wasn't sure it did go well with *Icecream* and was afraid it would somehow spoil it. But when we did *Hot Fudge* as a reading anyway we found we liked it. So now I feel the two plays can be done either together or separately.

Caryl Churchill, 1989

LOVESICK

Characters

HODGE
MAX
ELLEN
ROBERT
KEVIN
JESSICA

Lovesick was broadcast on BBC Radio 3 on 8 April 1967. The cast was as follows:

HODGE	Anthony Hall
MAX	Harold Kasket
ELLEN	Gudrun Ure
ROBERT	Ian Thompson
KEVIN	Clive Merrison
JESSICA	Margaret Robertson

Produced by John Tydeman

HODGE. When Smith raped he didn't find what he was looking for, so then he dissected with a chopper and was left with a face and meat to stuff in a sack. I cured Smith. But I could dissect Ellen, not so crudely, not even surgically, but in the laboratory applying every known stimulus to that organism and getting all her reactions by analysis, by hypnosis, by abreactive drugs, by shaving her red hair and laying bare her brain, yes, surgery perhaps or a chopper.
McNab, Ellen, age thirty, married, three children. Depressed, not seriously, obvious causes.

ELLEN My husband was always sure I'd be unfaithful. At first I used to say, No, no I won't.

HODGE. And so Kevin, Zolotov, Kevin, age twenty-five, loved by Ellen McNab against probability one might think, considering asthma, bitten nails, constipation perhaps, certainly his breath often smelt. People with commonplace interpretations of appearance would have thought at once that he was homosexual.

KEVIN. I've been a Catholic, Hodge, I've been a Buddhist. I wish I'd been born a Jew. Having the race I might have stuck to the beliefs.

HODGE. Zolotov, Zolotov, Robert, brother of Kevin above. I can get hold of Kevin if I'm careful to be objective, but Robert – shadows under his eyes.

ROBERT. You're a psychiatrist are you, Dr Hodge? Do you find it fun?

HODGE. Zolotov, Jessica, divorced, mother of Robert and Kevin q.v.

JESSICA. I'm sure you could help us, Dr Hodge.

HODGE. There was a time before I knew them. I hardly noticed first hearing of Ellen McNab, the woman in love with Kevin Zolotov. And I was delighted with the Zolotovs the day Max took me to meet them, boasting of his affair with the mother. Max, an old friend I should know well, Brown Max, age forty, married, car dealer, physical condition too good and, of course, timid eyes. I sat back in his latest old Jaguar, his black alsatians behind me, and enjoyed the ride.

MAX   I'd rather be up against a husband than two sons. It's about time they cleared out as well. How can I be alone with Jessica? She says she can't help worrying about them. It's very sweet of her but I'm the one who should be worried, I'm the one who's married. I'm responsible for poor Lucy. And I'm responsible for Jessica, they both love me. What can I do? I lie awake half the night.

HODGE.   You don't want to do that.

MAX.   If you could keep the boys happy a bit this afternoon, Hodge. They're old enough to mind their own business.

HODGE.   Kevin was sitting in the apple tree, so casually that I was sure his attractive position was contrived.

KEVIN.   Well if it isn't Max. And who's your friend?

HODGE.   Robert appeared to be asleep on the grass for longer than seemed likely.

ROBERT.   Keep your dogs off, Max. You know they don't like us.

JESSICA.   Oh Max, we're so glad to see you. You mustn't mind the boys, Dr Hodge. Come down, Kevin, and shake hands. They'll get us a drink, won't you darlings. Kevin. Robert. Don't scuffle like that. Dr Hodge will think you're complete children.

HODGE.   The situation seemed clear enough. I've seen possessive mothers before. Jessica lay in a striped deckchair while she and Max fought the young men, and I found it amusing after a week's work.

JESSICA.   Max has told us about your fascinating work, Dr Hodge.

KEVIN.   Max said it was balls.

MAX.   It is too and downright immoral, but that's all right, Hodge knows I'm not clever like him.

JESSICA.   I'm going to tell Ellen to recommend Dr Hodge to her aunt. Do you know Ellen McNab? She's got a husband and a drunken aunt but she has her points. I always defend the poor girl against my boys. Kevin's so finicky.

KEVIN.   You can't stand her.

JESSICA.   She'd make you an excellent wife if she wasn't married. She'd leave her husband you know Dr Hodge, if Kevin asked her. She'd bring the children of course.

MAX.   But Kevin loves little boys, don't you, Kevin?

KEVIN.   Have you and Lucy any children, Max? No? Keep trying.

JESSICA.   You're a doctor, Dr Hodge, you can tell me why I can't get up in the morning. I feel it should be a matter of will-power but really it's more like an illness.

ROBERT.   You enjoy sleep, nobody needs you awake, why not let Dr Hodge enjoy his drink?

JESSICA.   Robert's so rude, no wonder he's got no girlfriends. I sometimes despair of getting rid of my sons.

HODGE.   It was that day, on Kevin's transistor that he played too loudly for us to talk, that news of a hurricane killing several hundred coincided with the discovery of a mutilated body, one of Smith's first victims. Max, of course, wanted the death penalty or worse, while I explained at length the possibilities of cure. Even Jessica sided with me and we all laughed at Max.

ROBERT.   If he wants to punish killers he'd better go to

Florida. Can't you see Max flogging the wind?

HODGE.   That must be what gave me the idea that Robert
was interested in my work. I went on talking
and Max took Jessica away to show him the
garden. Soon I realised Robert and Kevin were
whispering like children in class and they crept
off after Max and Jessica. I got myself another
drink and enjoyed the evening sun. Suddenly
Robert and Kevin ran past, laughing, with Max
chasing them, red faced and serious.

JESSICA.   The dogs. Look out. Robert.

The sound of dogs barking.

HODGE.   Robert turned a hose on Max, who staggered,
waving his arms and trying to go on running.
Then the alsatians knocked Robert over. I
remember Kevin laughing even harder at that,
while Jessica screamed. Max was holding a
lunging dog by the collar in each hand, pulled
from side to side, blind with water, and
swearing, while the hose jumped about by itself.
Robert got up, his clothes torn and his hand
bleeding. Kevin giggled from his tree. Jessica
ran up and slapped Robert's face and they
started to quarrel so loudly that I couldn't
understand a word, and I went and sat in the
car and waited for Max. He drove me back to
the hospital and then went home to his wife,
Lucy, a little woman dressed in flowers.
I'm used to writing case histories and colleagues
admire the clarity of my style. Ten thousand
words on Ellen McNab was too much so it went
into the wastepaper basket.
McNab, Ellen, when I met her was the niece of a
patient whom I was curing with a drug that
causes nausea at the taste of alcohol. Jessica had
recommended me as she said, but I'd forgotten
that and didn't connect the girl with the
Zolotovs. McNab, Ellen, married, I saw her
hand, was slumped on her aunt's untidy bed.
Her red hair fell forward and hid most of her
face, so I walked round to straighten the pillows

and see more than her rather dirty nostrils. I
dropped a pillow to get close to her legs, which
she hadn't shaved for at least a fortnight. 'What
if you have cured me,' said the aunt, 'what do I
do now? I like drinking, it's my only hobby.'
'Nonsense,' I said, tucking her in, this is a
depressing stage. It wasn't Ellen's dirt and
ugliness that attracted me but her beauty, which
must have been great to outweigh them.
I'm reminded of a tall boy at school who got
dressed most mornings in dirty clothes, swore at
me in a way I didn't dare imitate till ten years
later, and once pushed me into a canal. I wasn't
at all frightened as I fell in; the water was cold
just as I expected, and I swam to the bank in
great excitement. I was standing there, shivering
and watching him, when a dog stopped to sniff
at my wet clothes and knocked me off balance.
For a moment it seemed I would fall into the
canal again. My back ached for hours from the
twist I gave to stumble on to the towpath, and it
is this second fall into the canal, which never
happened, that frightened me and comes back
in dreams or most times when I miss my
footing.

ELLEN.   Tell me about your work.

HODGE.   For a long time now Ellen and my work have
been inseparable because my fantasies kept her
with me all the time. Watching white rats solve
their mazes, I seemed to be craning into Ellen's
mind. Walking in the clinic garden the first day
we met she asked me about my work, to stop me
asking her questions or being silent. So I talked
about Pavlov and thought either she must know
it already or else it's too specialised to be
interesting. My answer to both worries was to
clown. The dog sees the food and salivates,
slurp, slurp; now we ring a bell and show food,
ding, slurp; now we ring a bell without food,
now you see the conditioned reflex, ding, slurp,
even without food the poor dog drools. I was up
to my ankles in leaves.

ELLEN.   I must catch my bus.

HODGE.   You can give a dog a nervous breakdown by
           teaching it a positive reaction to a circle and a
           negative one to an oval. Gradually you show it
           more and more compressed ovals.

ELLEN.   I don't like the woman who's looking after the
           children.

HODGE.   I'm sure you're very happily married.

ELLEN.   No. But I'm in love with someone else.

HODGE.   She must have been as tense as me because we
           howled with laughter. I realised she was the
           woman who was in love with Kevin Zolotov. Just
           then a nymphomaniac walked by, a seventeen-
           year-old patient who should have been locked
           up. She was a plump girl with mousy hair and
           glasses, and unsuspecting schoolboys, teachers,
           librarians, doctors, priests, business
           acquaintances of her father's, perhaps her father
           himself, had found themselves cornered by this
           dowdy child, till her parents had sent her to me.
           I remembered the gardener was sweeping leaves
           behind us so I had to walk back to the building
           with her. She kept weaving close to me and
           putting her fingers against my thigh so that I
           had to keep my thoughts firmly on her spotty
           face and near insanity. And perhaps it was Ellen
           who was entirely responsible for my distress
           when I was alone at last in my white room with
           my dog Pavlova, to whom I've resisted the
           temptation to give a nervous breakdown. But
           when I'd spent some time in the lavatory I felt
           quite well enough to make my evening rounds.
           Zolotov, Kevin, danced well alone, which I once
           saw at a party, and worked for a firm that made
           shampoo. He once showed me some of his bad
           poetry. None of this explains why Ellen was in
           love with him, which I wondered all night after
           finding them looking embarrassed together in
           the bathroom at Ellen's where she was helping
           him take an eyelash out of his eye. It was hard

to make occasions to see Ellen and I spent as much time as I could at the Zolotovs', where I ate big meals in my own place opposite Kevin. Avidly I watched his mouth that had kissed Ellen, now full of brandy cake and flecked with cream like mine. Zolotov, Robert. I didn't notice him enough. I find it hard to concentrate on him. When Kevin went out I followed him to his little room where he sat alone with stuffed animals and stamp collections, reading books that would have interested me had I had time, and talked about my work. He understood everything at once, and when he complained about the dullness of his work in a bank I suggested almost seriously that he should give it up and work with me. I was hurt for a moment by the way he looked at me, with disgust I think, and laughed. But I'd always known he disliked me for my friendship with Max, so I laughed with him and didn't worry about it. I didn't even dislike Kevin. All the time I spent there seemed time spent with Ellen.

MAX.   You could have Ellen.

HODGE.   Max on Hampstead Heath as we walked Pavlova and his black alsatians.

MAX.   Kevin's queer.

HODGE.   Max shadow boxing, lifting weights, standing on his head.

MAX.   What more do you want? Kevin's –

HODGE.   No no, no, he just looks it.

MAX.   Jessica tells me all about it. It's a hell of a thing for a woman to have a son like that.

HODGE.   She'd love it.

MAX.   He even says he'll leave home and move in with his friend. I don't say this to Jessica but I wish he would and take Robert with him. Last night they were both out for once and we were up in Jessica's room. Suddenly we hear somebody coming upstairs. Everything stops. Jessica sits up. She even had me worried, I grabbed the bedside lamp to hit him with. Then she says, it's Robert. I put down the lamp, everything's all right – but no, she puts her hand over my mouth. And Robert stops outside the bedroom door. I bit her hand, she swore, I had to laugh. It's carrying modesty a bit too far, her sons aren't children, they've got to accept that their mother's a woman. Jessica sees that, because she said very loudly, 'Leave the hall light on, Robert, so Max can see his way down later on.' Then he turned the light off and went to his room. But the joy had gone out of it all by then.

HODGE.   Does Lucy know about Jessica?

MAX.   Lucy? I don't know. We never speak. She's always on her hands and knees following the dogs to clean their paw-marks off. Or else knitting me sweaters, very fast. Neither of us can get a word in. She spends two hours in the kitchen and when dinner is ready I go out, I'd choke on it. She's got plenty of clothes but we never go anywhere. So she spends the evening trying them on in front of the mirror. I come home at one and find her in pink silk with a blue feather toque, sitting on a kitchen stool drinking cocoa. Of course I feel guilty but what can I do? So I take the dogs out for a last pee.

HODGE.   I hardly bothered to explain Max to myself. Alsatians and Jessica were clearly compensations for unadmitted doubts of his masculinity. I dealt with him too easily, I didn't expect him to change, and anyway I had other things to think about.
There was a time when things were going well. I cured the dowdy nymphomaniac much as I cured Ellen's aunt. First she was given a drug which causes nausea and then photographs of naked men. I wasn't sure if photographs would be enough so at a later stage I put my

extraordinarily unquestioning and really stupid assistant Jenks into her room and told him to undress. To my delight she vomited repeatedly. The skilful part was modifying the effects so that she just trembled with entirely suitable modesty when Jenks, apparently spontaneously, kissed her shyly on the cheek the day she went home. Her engagement to a curate was announced a few months later. A spy tells me he found her a little cold at first but is proudly changing that. Another remarkable cure was Smith, the rapist and murderer. The papers were full of his mutilated victims but to my joy he came to me before the police knew anything about him. Max wanted me to castrate him but my usual method was perfectly successful, leaving only a slight distaste for sex and butchers in an otherwise well-balanced personality. He is back at work, the joy, as always, of his old parents, and my only worry is that the police may yet catch him and hold him responsible for his corpses.

An unexpected patient was Jessica Zolotov, who was admitted to my clinic suffering from an attempt to hang herself. She was found at once, as she might have expected, by Max, who propped her beside him in an Alfa-Romeo and brought her to me for friendship and privacy.

MAX.   I blame myself Hodge.

HODGE.   No no no.

MAX.   If she dies it will be a judgement on me. A punishment for the pain I've caused Lucy. If I hadn't been so insistent, I see that now, this would never –

HODGE.   There's no need for you to feel responsible.

MAX.   But you see, I wanted –

HODGE.   Of course you did. Don't get up.

MAX.   No one could blame me for loving Jessica.

HODGE.   That's the spirit. You can't help being yourself. I
          could have told you this would happen, if only
          I'd known a bit more about you both, and taken
          steps to prevent it. We'll make sure it doesn't
          happen again. Now have you any idea why she –

MAX.   Because she loves me. You know human nature,
          Hodge. She's frightened by her passion for me,
          that's it. She's been alone so long. Hodge, I've
          got this terrible feeling of guilt.

HODGE.   Drink this –

MAX.   If she's punished –

HODGE.   Suicide's not a crime any more. Sit quietly,
          there's a good chap.

MAX.   But is it still a sin, that's the point. I'm an
          outdoor man, this isn't my line at all, but a thing
          like that knocks you back. If she goes to hell it's
          me put her there.

HODGE.   Jessica Zolotov was soon out of danger and
          unfortunately discharged herself before I could
          give her any further treatment. She nodded to
          me and walked down the steps, looking older
          than she usually manages to, and leaning on the
          arm of her son, Robert. I could certainly have
          helped her if she'd stayed.
          It was about this time, full of myself, that I
          decided to act on Max's assurance that I could
          have Ellen. I went to see her.

          A child cries.

ELLEN.   I'm afraid I smack him if he wets himself. He's
          old enough to know.

HODGE.   You should smack him before he does it, it's a
          better deterrent.

ELLEN.   Fine.

HODGE.   Or do you just want to punish him because you
          feel he's guilty.

ELLEN.   I do it because I'm cross, all right?

HODGE. Ellen, I've something to tell you.

ELLEN. What? Keep still, darling, let me get your trousers off.

HODGE. It's about Kevin. He's homosexual. He's thinking of going to live with a man –

ELLEN. Yes, that's right. What did you want to tell me?

HODGE. You know it all then. I just wondered.

ELLEN. There, that's better, all dry now. The man's called Michael and he's coming to lunch.

HODGE. Aren't you jealous?

ELLEN. Yes, we're both jealous. We both think Kevin's going to change.

HODGE. He won't change. He's a common type of mother-dominated – you can smile. You don't want him to change. You've deliberately chosen a homosexual. You deliberately married a boring middle-aged Scot who seemed completely remote from you. You don't want relationships that work. You know why you love Kevin, don't you? Because you're afraid of sex, that's all. And why he loves you, that's just as easy to explain – you're like his mother. She married a Russian completely remote from her, and she got rid of him and lives for her children just as you do. Kevin can go on being a child with you. So much for your loving –

ELLEN. Kevin's coming to lunch as well as Michael. Do you think I won't tell them everything you say? And we'll all laugh at you, Dr Hodge.

HODGE. Ellen's apparent dislike of me is a defence because she knows I understand her. Her slovenliness is explained by her fear of sex. It's not dirt that attracts me but her beauty, which must be great – I'm a tidy man, I can't help it. It wouldn't be careless of me to forget to collect my shirts from the laundry or to put on dirty socks, it would be contrived. In any case there's nothing about my smooth face with its short nose and pale close-set eyes to stand out against the mess, while in a neat inconspicuous setting I am at least visible. After that visit to Ellen, seeing Robert and Kevin was a waste of time. I was closer to Ellen alone, working and thinking about her. They can't have missed me when I stopped dropping in, but Jessica claimed to, the day she came to see me.

JESSICA.   Couldn't you help Kevin, Dr Hodge? Make him normal?

HODGE.   She had changed since her attempted suicide. She was more relaxed and didn't see Max any more. Max was evasive.

MAX.   I had a talk with Lucy. For one thing I've got rid of the alsatians – a bit childish really, big dogs. I got a good home for the little one, but I had to have the old one put down, he was a one-man dog. You won't believe it but I cried over that. Well I managed to tell Lucy a lot of things. She bought me this shirt, do you like it? The thing is I had a talk with Robert.

HODGE.   It was a pink silk shirt, unusual for Max, but I wasn't interested in his clothes and it was a long time before I went to his house and saw Lucy. I was too busy with my plans for Kevin. Jessica wanted me to cure him of homosexuality and my first thought was to do the opposite. I'd give him the nausea drug all right and follow it not with pictures of men but with pictures of Ellen, and other women too for good measure. I'd rehabilitate him in love with Michael and ·disgusted by Ellen, leaving her for me. But it seemed a bit unfair to Jessica and more important would make Ellen angry with me. No, I would cure Kevin after all, but at the same time make sure I got Ellen. Jessica and Ellen persuaded Kevin to have treatment. Ellen may not have believed me when I told her she was near a nervous breakdown and needed a rest in the clinic herself, but luckily she liked the idea of being close to Kevin. It was settled that they would come together. Then I went to the photographer's. I decided to have a holiday during their treatment. Kevin's was routine, and though Ellen's was more experimental, I didn't see how I could both administer the experiment and in my photographs be part of it without jeopardising the result. So I had to leave them with Jenks, and to avoid the strain of passing Ellen's closed door day after day I decided to go right away. I saw them both settled in their rooms and went to pack. Robert Zolotov came to see me.

ROBERT.   What are you doing to Kevin?

HODGE.   Curing him.

ROBERT.   He's not ill.

HODGE.   He's homosexual.

ROBERT.   Yes, and he's got brown eyes, so what?

HODGE.   I'm not criticising your brother, Robert. He's not responsible for the hereditary and environmental factors that determine his condition. Max would like the sin of sodomy punished but you and I know better than that, I think.

ROBERT.   Don't we know enough to leave him alone?

HODGE.   You want him to have a normal happy life.

ROBERT.   I don't much care what happens to Kevin. He does me what little harm he can. Sibling rivalry. No, go ahead if you want to. I'm more curious about Ellen.

HODGE.   Ellen?

ROBERT.   She's here for – what, exactly?

HODGE.   A rest.

ROBERT.   Before going to live with Kevin.

HODGE.   If your mother lets him.

ROBERT.   She wants Kevin to marry Ellen. She wants him

	happy and out of the way.
HODGE.	I don't think you understand your mother.
ROBERT.	Of course I understand Jessica, Hodge. I'm sure you realise you'll never have Ellen.
HODGE.	I've been asked to cure your brother. It's a routine matter. My personal feelings don't come into it.
ROBERT.	But Hodge, you're up to something much more clever. What are you doing to Ellen?
HODGE.	I like you, Robert.
ROBERT.	Well never mind. I'm sure you can explain it away just as you can my dislike for you.
HODGE.	We haven't got on. But at least you're perceptive. I respect you. You'll respect me in a minute. My assistant Jenks is a fool, he just does what he's told, he gets no pleasure from our experiments. I've no one to share them with and I do sometimes long – it's brilliant, Robert. I'm going to cure her of Kevin. I'll make her feel disgusted at the sight of him for the rest of her life. Then I'll cure her phobia for me, that's easy enough. And then I'll addict her to me. She won't be able to live without me. She'll experience almost physical pain when I withdraw and the most intense well-being and ecstasy when I'm with her. She'll beg me to stay with her. I'm not surprised you don't say anything. I sometimes dare to hope I have genius. No relationship is beyond my help. I could do a lot for you. Would you like me to detach you a little from your mother? Not make you hate her, just set you right. Perhaps you don't realise it, but you and Kevin have a very possessive mother. You're both jealous of Max, you've driven him away, I gather. That's because – in your unconsciousness of course, it's not uncommon – you want to sleep with your mother.
ROBERT.	I do.

HODGE.

Yes, well done, Robert, face it, you do want to, and more strongly than is quite normal. That's what's behind Kevin's homosexuality –

ROBERT.

I mean I do sleep with her.

HODGE.

All my troubles are due to Robert Zolotov. I sacked my assistant Jenks when I found what part he played in the fiasco but I've never had any revenge on Robert and the idea was certainly his. Jenks was merely stupid, and too used to strange cures to object when Robert pretended he had an urgent message from me to change the treatments for Kevin and Ellen. I left for my holiday irritated with Robert for being so opposed to my cures, especially for himself. He just said he loved Jessica and we finished up shouting at each other. His incest explained a great deal, of course. Jessica's suicide attempt was clearly caused by the strain of trying to break with Robert in his own interests and take up with Max, whom she didn't love. And Robert got rid of Max by telling him all about it. That night Lucy heard a noise and came downstairs to find Max sitting in the kitchen.

MAX.

I was sitting in the kitchen wearing her pink silk dress and blue toque. We do laugh when we think how we felt. I told her about Jessica and what Robert had just told me, and how I was lying in bed afterwards when I suddenly knew what I really wanted to do and I got up and got dressed like that. I do the housework, she always hated it – I never knew that, but now she can tell me – and I have the dinner ready for when she comes home from work. I didn't know I could just be myself. And it's so lucky we're married to each other. She's as happy as I am, and she's just bought six trouser suits.

HODGE.

When the cure should have been working I came back from my holiday. I visited Kevin first, wondering if his new aversion from men would apply to me. Perhaps not very strongly, I thought, since he hadn't found me attractive in the first place. He threw himself into my arms.

KEVIN. Don't let me see myself in the mirror. Do I disgust you too? Don't look at me or you'll never love me. Don't back away, hold me, hold me.

HODGE. I ran to see what had happened to Ellen. She wouldn't speak to me till I'd given up and was stumbling out of the room.

ELLEN. Doctor.

HODGE. Yes.

ELLEN. Send the nurse in to see me now.

HODGE. I don't know if Jessica's love for Robert meant she wasn't angry with him for swapping the cures. Instead of being cured of homosexuality, Kevin hated Kevin and loved me, as Ellen should have done. Certainly Jessica found it funny that Ellen had Kevin's cure and is now disgusted by men. I said I'd do Kevin again.

KEVIN. Cure me? What do you mean? I've always loved you. I used to be so annoyed by your knowing talk and now I see that was just a defence against my true feelings. I know I make you unhappy when I talk like that, I hate myself, but I can't help it, you're so wonderful.

HODGE. I might have persuaded him to have treatment, he loved me enough to do anything for me. More than anyone else has ever done. But I was too disheartened to start again at once and he killed himself before I got down to it. What Jessica must think now I don't know, I haven't spoken to her since. I hope Robert feels guilty. Kevin's self-disgust was pitiful but no one could blame me for not loving him. I've homosexual tendencies like anyone else, but well suppressed, and it was most inconvenient to have them stirred. Suicide clearly runs in the family. If only I could cure Ellen, but she won't come near me.

ELLEN. What do you mean I'm not really a lesbian? I

love her, I've never been so happy. Listen, I've
had dreams about women for years. And doesn't
it fit with my not liking men to choose old
Douglas and Kevin, who hardly liked touching
me?

HODGE.   When I was six I went to a fortune-teller who
told me I would die at the age of forty-seven.
That made me forget everything else she said,
so I can't check how accurate she was. I'm a
doctor and don't believe in such rubbish.
Possibly I became a doctor in order not to
believe in such rubbish. If I did believe it I
might well drop dead at forty-seven. I need
more than ten years to complete my work but
perhaps without Ellen I want to die, enough
anyway to remember the fortune-teller. I'm not
the type to commit suicide. There is an
alternative. Last week I thought I would call on
Robert and Jessica. From the gate I could see
them in the garden. Jessica was lying in a
deckchair and Robert on the grass. I was about
to go in when I saw that they were looking at
each other. I waited a moment but they didn't
move. They weren't smiling, it was more a look
of wonder, and it seemed I would have to wait a
long time. So I came away, and I won't bother
with them any more. I have a photograph of
Ellen on my desk. I've plenty more, and I will
take the drug in just a minute. It can't be fear of
nausea that makes me hesitate. By next week, if
I don't turn back, I could be free to concentrate
on my work, with no thought of Ellen, whose
beauty is great.

ABORTIVE

Characters

ROZ
COLIN

Abortive was first broadcast on BBC Radio 3, 4 February 1971. The cast was as follows:

ROZ	Prunella Scales
COLIN	Dinsdale Landen

Directed by John Tydeman

ROZ and COLIN are in bed. Silence. COLIN sighs heavily.

COLIN.	Just not on at all? Mm?
ROZ.	I'm sorry, Colin.
COLIN.	Not a bit. No no. Odd if it wasn't like this.
ROZ.	I still like to snuggle up. Do you mind?
COLIN.	My darling Roz, I'm not a monster.
ROZ.	It's only three weeks ago.
COLIN.	Are you warm enough without the blankets?
ROZ.	I'm too hot.
COLIN.	I know it's only three weeks, my pet.
ROZ.	In fact abortion is overrated. Men make it such a melodramatic topic. The backstreet aspect. It was bliss physically. The anaesthetic alone was worth the price. I quite understand why Billy took drugs.
COLIN.	Nevertheless it is a shock to the system.
ROZ.	It won't have made me permanently frigid.
COLIN.	I never for a moment –
ROZ.	Yes you did.
COLIN.	Unless of course you've stopped loving me.
ROZ.	Are you starting that? I wondered how long it would take.
COLIN.	Well it wasn't rape.
ROZ.	It started as rape. I might as well have lied to you about it. There was no need to tell you how it ended.
COLIN.	No need.
ROZ.	But you said that night in the garden when you found me – are you going to say you don't remember? You were leaning against a tree. You said we'd go on as if it hadn't happened. I

thought that was so beautiful. Our relationship was on a higher plane.

She starts to cry but tries to stop almost at once. A pause while she sobs and snuffles.

COLIN.   I saw Billy while you were in hospital.

ROZ.   Saw him?

COLIN.   He dropped into the office.

ROZ.   What happened?

COLIN.   He came to ask if you were all right.

ROZ.   I wonder what he was after. Were you polite?

COLIN.   I blame myself for having brought him here. It was unintelligent. One should have out-grown that sort of thing. Nights I work late by myself my eyes get tired, I have a few drinks. I'm more receptive to the beauties of nature but I've seen the scenes before. One hopes for something different. I'd just missed a train, I was somewhat annoyed. It was relaxing to strike up a conversation with a friendly chap from a different walk of life and clearly not stupid. Our chat took quite a philosophical turn. One should leave well alone.

ROZ.   You liked him.

COLIN.   He had a charm, it serves a purpose. It earned him three months' keep and our attention. It was gross self-indulgence on my part to think a man of forty could change.

ROZ.   Thirty-seven.

COLIN.   Bound to be set – what?

ROZ.   Nothing.

COLIN.   Thirty-seven?

ROZ.   Of course he was set in his ways. He enjoyed it though. He was grateful to you for bringing him to the country. He did enjoy it in the beginning.

COLIN.   I suppose one can't stifle all one's impulses. I wouldn't help someone again.

ROZ.   You've always been too kind. I've said this before. People take advantage. I don't know why your wife and children aren't enough. You can be kind to us.

COLIN.   I did have inklings in my youth of the unity as it were of things. If such indeed exists I appear to be excluded from it. My efforts to join take the form of pity.

ROZ.   Billy had quite enough pity for himself. As if anyone noticed he was one-quarter coloured.

COLIN.   Half.

ROZ.   I thought his father was half.

COLIN.   He distinctly told me the first night on the station his father was black.

ROZ.   He never saw him so he wouldn't know.

COLIN.   His father used to visit them sometimes.

ROZ.   He never told me.

COLIN.   He used to beat Billy up. You remember the story about when he was thrown out of the window. You've told it yourself at dinner.

ROZ.   I thought that was the Irishman. His so-called stepfather.

COLIN.   No, it was his father. He used to come and see them when he was drunk.

ROZ.   I thought he was blind, Paddy.

COLIN.   How could a blind man throw him out of the window?

ROZ.   Paddy certainly used to beat him up.

COLIN.   Perhaps he was only blind in one eye.

They are laughing by now. They stop.

He certainly told us a lot of lies.

ROZ.   His mother –

COLIN.   (*impatiently*). Oh!

            Pause. It is windy outside. The curtains are blowing.

ROZ.   How windy it is tonight. And we still can't
            breathe.

COLIN.   Shall I open the curtains?

ROZ.   You can try it.

COLIN.   (*getting up to open the curtains*). Is Ingrid getting
            the children up in the morning?

ROZ.   Yes, but they'll cry.

COLIN.   Ingrid's incompetent.

ROZ.   She's not as good as Yvonne.

COLIN.   Wasn't I right to send Yvonne away? As it
            turned out?

ROZ.   You mean you'd rather your wife was raped
            than the au pair girl.

COLIN.   I mean he was the kind of bastard I thought.

ROZ.   Yvonne led him on. They'd take the children to
            romp in the field and she'd play ring a roses
            with Ellie and stay fallen down. I hardly liked
            Ellie to be involved. I like to think of the open
            air as healthy. I used to see them from the
            window.

COLIN.   I'm sure you did.

ROZ.   Well Ingrid's got bigger bosoms than Yvonne so
            you've done all right.

COLIN.   When do I look at Ingrid?

ROZ.   She looks at you.

COLIN.   I hadn't noticed.

ROZ.   I wouldn't blame you.

COLIN.   Ingrid's not at all the type of girl –

ROZ. But there is a type –

COLIN. What?

ROZ. There is a type of girl you fancy.

COLIN. You.

ROZ. But fifteen years younger. If I went on not feeling up to it. We've understood for a long time what you get from me, I've no head. I don't understand what you do all day. You haven't managed to make me read.

COLIN. You're morbid.

ROZ. You would have felt too guilty before. So nothing's ever come to anything. But now you feel you've a right.

COLIN. Nonsense.

ROZ. You feel things aren't the same.

COLIN. They're not the same. (*Pause.*) I suppose I can't say what I might do.

Pause. Wind and rain outside. COLIN *is standing looking out of the window.*

ROZ. Raining at last. It may get cooler. Come back to bed.

COLIN. It's a splendid night. The trees tossing about and so forth. It makes the commuting worth while. The nights in town make one more sensitive to nature. The air's quite a different quality. And now a weekend at last. We'll get you better.

ROZ. Do you hate him?

COLIN. Billy?

ROZ. Do you hate him?

COLIN. One can see both sides.

ROZ. I'm sure we both began to hate him when you had to send Yvonne away.

COLIN.   I'd given up trying to talk to him by then.

ROZ.   But fancy depending on Billy for domestic help. Everyone said the same, I was quite right to lose my temper.

COLIN.   One shouldn't expect too much.

ROZ.   He'd start whatever I wanted quite sweetly but never finish. Not that he had anything better to do. He followed me about. If people came to tea he stayed in the room.

COLIN.   He was essentially boring.

ROZ.   I was quite prepared to treat him as a friend but what return did I get?

COLIN.   The whole episode was one more mistake.

ROZ.   But he was at his most utterly loathsome when we'd finally kicked him out and he didn't have the decency to leave the area, all that time at the end, right up.

COLIN.   That was unforgiveable. I must say.

ROZ.   I still feel faint if the phone rings.

COLIN.   I know it's not in the realms of possibility to find him leaning against the carpark wall but I still flinch when I come out of the station. He must have wasted an inordinate amount of time because he can't have known which train I was on or even which day. And yet I could always count on his being there.

ROZ.   I never spoke to him at that time.

COLIN.   Even when I made it perfectly clear by ignoring him. Even when I said quite loudly, 'Go away Billy'. A dog would have obeyed. Stumbling after me to the car, distorting his face against the window, pleading with me quite unintelligibly since I couldn't hear a word through the glass.

ROZ.   He'd suddenly be there beside me when I was going shopping and wait outside every shop. I had to take the car.

COLIN.	He got us a bad name in the village.
ROZ.	I used to see him from the window sleeping in the field.
COLIN.	We should have called the police.
ROZ.	He used to come into the garden.
COLIN.	I did begin to fear for your safety.
ROZ.	I was never frightened, I was angry. Not to be able to walk under my own trees.

Pause. Wind and rain outside.

All out of love for us, he claimed, that was what really got me, love for us.

COLIN.	He hated us.
ROZ.	He was envious.
COLIN.	One is more lucky than most people.
ROZ.	Lucky? I think we've suffered fantastically.
COLIN.	I meant materially. The house, the area, the way of life. The children.
ROZ.	At least he didn't hurt the children.
COLIN.	It hasn't been the worst possible.
ROZ.	He was even fond of Ellie in his way.
COLIN.	I would have killed him.
ROZ.	At least we never saw him again.
COLIN.	He came into the office.
ROZ.	I don't count that. I haven't seen him.
COLIN.	Do you feel at all that you love him?
ROZ.	Of course I don't.
COLIN.	Not at all?
ROZ.	No.
COLIN.	No.

ROZ.   You're not going to start thinking that?

COLIN.   No.

ROZ.   But you are.

COLIN.   It happened.

ROZ.   Because he hated us.

COLIN.   But at the end you didn't struggle.

ROZ.   You know how things can be.

            Pause. Wind and rain.

            You know yourself you had that moment on the
            station in London the night you brought him
            down. You kept me awake so late while you
            explained. You'd had this moment of feeling
            close to him and rational considerations
            dropped away. They were your words. But that
            moment seems nothing now. You said to him at
            the time, 'You can count on me.'

COLIN.   And now?

ROZ.   What now?

COLIN.   You feel indifferent towards him? Would you
            say?

ROZ.   That can't be right.

COLIN.   He doesn't seem some sort of ideal lover? He
            might. You might have a fixation, if you
            understand the term.

ROZ.   I haven't. I can imagine how I would feel if I
            did feel what you say. There was a time when
            we both liked him. And possibly I have a
            sentimental . . . the father of my child, that
            feeling, though of course it wasn't a child. But
            it's not entirely sentimental to say it would have
            been a child. No more than that.

COLIN.   How can I help being jealous?

ROZ.   You said you wouldn't be.

COLIN.   How can I help it?

ROZ.   Because I can't bear it.

COLIN.   You wish you'd had his child.

ROZ.   Of course I didn't want his degenerate child.

COLIN.   You could have kept it, I told you at the time. I
          would have accepted it as a child of the family.

ROZ.   And loved it like Ellie? And what would people
          have said? Even the law says it's right in the case
          of rape.

COLIN.   It wasn't rape.

ROZ.   It was as good as rape. (*She gets out of bed.*)

COLIN.   Now where are you going?

ROZ.   Just going.

COLIN.   Now Roz, come back here.

ROZ.   Going out.

          She goes out to the garden.
          COLIN *stays in the room.*

COLIN.   Roz.

ROZ.   Going away.

COLIN.   Roz.

ROZ.   Somewhere.

          She is now in the garden.

          Ah yes. Out.

          She stands for some time as if in the rain.
          COLIN *comes quietly behind her.*

COLIN.   Roz.

ROZ.   You frightened me.

COLIN.   You're beautiful.

ROZ.   Oh you frightened me.

COLIN.   Your hair, I can wring it.

ROZ.   I never thought you'd come after me.

COLIN.   I have my moments.

ROZ.   Are you happy?

COLIN.   Yes, and you are.

ROZ.   Yes.

COLIN.   We'll be all right.

ROZ.   Of course we are.

COLIN.   My Roz, come in.

ROZ.   Must we?

COLIN.   Come in to bed.

ROZ.   Is it nice?

COLIN.   I'll make you warm.

ROZ.   We're so wet.

           They start to go in.

COLIN.   The footprints. Ingrid –

ROZ.   Ingrid will think it was a burglar.

COLIN.   Barefoot.

ROZ.   Dripping.

COLIN.   Hush, we'll wake her.

ROZ.   Or the children, worse.

COLIN.   Hush then.

           They come into the bedroom.

ROZ.   Oh oh look at me, how wet.

COLIN.   Here's a towel.

ROZ.   How happy we are sometimes.

COLIN.   I'll dry your hair.

ROZ.   We're together again. Oh but kiss me.

They kiss.

COLIN.   There now. Come, let me dry your hair.

ROZ.   But you're sad all of a sudden.

COLIN.   No.

ROZ.   You are.

COLIN.   No.

ROZ.   Yes, don't lie about it.

COLIN.   It's all been so unpleasant.

ROZ.   But you wanted to make love. It was me that didn't.

COLIN.   It will come right in time.

ROZ.   But I thought you'd be so glad.

COLIN.   I would have thought so but it seems not.

ROZ.   I might as well have had the baby.

COLIN.   You see, you do want it.

ROZ.   I do miss something.

She cries.
COLIN *doesn't touch her, he lies on the bed. She goes on crying, then gradually stops. She lies down too. When she speaks she still has a catch in her breath.*

It was such a load off my mind when it was all over. Shall I tell you the best moment? Just before they give you the anaesthetic. Perhaps it's even better to look back on because at the time I was a little frightened. The doctors hardly look like people because you can't see their heads properly. They're covered from head to foot with light green equipment except their eyes. It's a bit like something underwater. So you lie there on your narrow table with a pleasant floating sensation from the first injection you had downstairs and you know that in a minute you'll be gone. Not asleep, you know it can't be like sleep at all because I'm alive to anything that happens when I'm asleep aren't I, a child only has to murmur. But in the case of the anaesthetic you know they'll be doing ghastly things to you in just a moment, but from your own point of view you won't be at all. You miss all the unpleasantness. Like being dead.

Pause. No wind or rain.

COLIN.   It's stopped raining. The wind's dropped.

ROZ.   We might have a blanket.

COLIN *pulls a blanket onto the bed, and lies back again.*

COLIN.   I do have one memory of Billy in the early days which isn't altogether painful. I usually find our picnics by the river somewhat routine. One goes of course for the children's benefit. One's own childhood picnics were a joy. You may remember the occasion. An April day, unprecedentedly hot, so we felt we must go out though I had brought a sizeable pile of work home. I believe I sat up late. An English scene so remarkable for its pale green that it seemed even at the time like a memory or indeed a photograph. We were hiring a large rowing boat with a wicker seat and ropes to steer with, and I'd just got in and was keeping it steady, and we helped the children down, and they sat still, and you got in, and Billy was hesitating on the bank in that old blue shirt of mine, and he didn't get in. He smiled and said, 'I've never been in a boat.' Then Ellie put up her hand and said, 'Come on, Billy, don't be frightened.' She'd been in a boat so many times you know, and only three. It brought tears to my eyes at the time.

ROZ.   He was certainly lying because he told me he'd worked his passage to South America.

Pause. It is lighter outside. A blackbird sings.

COLIN.   Ah, the birds.

A longer pause, while the dawn chorus begins. It goes on through ROZ's *next speech.*

ROZ.   What I shudder to think of is the night he came here, soon after we'd finally got him out of the house and I thought we were finally going to have some well-deserved peace. And then the telephone. He went on ringing the entire evening, I'll never forget it, there wasn't time to knit so much as one row between calls, crying and saying he was going to kill himself so we finally had to leave the phone off. And ten minutes later we heard the doorbell chime and I knew, that was the worst moment. You should never have let him in, it must have taken an hour to get him out. How can a grown man cry so much? What did he expect us to believe? That he'd really come to love us so much he couldn't bear to leave us? He was drunk. Or hooked on one of those ghastly drugs. So he finally made you pull him by the feet. I can see him now on his stomach clutching at everything he passed, at my ankles but I kicked him off, at the table leg, at the drawing-room door and of course he caught his fingers, stupid fool. All down the stairs clutching at the banisters, I'm quite surprised he didn't pull one out but he's not a strong man at all, and grabbed the coat rack in the hall so it crashed over, and all the time crying and saying 'please'. I thought he was going to wake the children. Out the front door at last, down the steps with a horrible bump, down the drive clutching furrows in the gravel till at last you got him outside the gate and dumped him on the grass verge. He must have enjoyed such a scene.

Dawn chorus ends during next speech. It is lighter.

COLIN.   You know when he came to see me in the office? We had a bit of a skirmish. It was very embarrassing in fact because of course it couldn't be kept quiet. The room was quite smashed up. Miss Hutchins came in and saw us and very wisely rang the police. By the time they came he was unconscious. They had to carry him off. I'll have to appear at his trial and give evidence.

ROZ.   You weren't hurt?

COLIN.   No, hardly at all.

ROZ.   It's getting light.

COLIN.   I suppose I really ought to draw the curtains. But nothing's going to stop me going to sleep. The light's not unpleasant.

He shuts his eyes. Pause. It goes on getting lighter.

ROZ.   I sleep badly now, don't I. It won't last. I have bad dreams. One night there was an explosion and I knew it had killed me. Everything was unsteady and far away and I must have been falling slowly to the ground. It was too late to think of you or the children or anything to do with staying alive. I thought yes, I don't mind dying if it's like this, if there's no pain, but let this be all, and I woke up. I dream of something violent every night. I dare say it's the operation. I never dream of Billy or the child. I sometimes think though, one of my children was so small, only an inch or so, so stupid, a mental age of eight weeks from conception, what sort of mind is that? Even less of a person than Billy. It's not only light now, there's actual sun and I'm still not asleep. It's going to be a nice hot day, that's a comfort. I do find I'm afraid to go to sleep. Just as I'm going off I get that feeling like in a nightmare but with no content. I'm frightened something's about to happen.

NOT NOT
NOT NOT NOT
ENOUGH OXYGEN

Characters

VIVIAN
MICK
CLAUDE

VIVIAN is 30. She dresses to look young but her face looks older, very pale and ill.
MICK is 60. He has dressed carefully in his best clothes.
CLAUDE is 19. He has very fair hair, cut short, and is beautiful. His clothes are expensive but crumpled and dusty.

The time is 2010. Mick was young in the seventies. Clothes shouldn't look space-age but different from contemporary ones. Mick perhaps likes the bright colours of his youth, now old-fashioned. Claude might wear a dark suit.

The place is Mick's one room in a tower block. It is small, brightly painted and very cluttered: bed, table, chairs, etc, including one large old-fashioned armchair; TV; music; books; games; puzzles; large jigsaw half finished on a table; jug of water and glasses; intercom by the door for speaking to the front door downstairs; one window, shut, looking out to smoggy sky.

Not Not Not Not Not Enough Oxygen was first broadcast on BBC Radio 3, 31 March 1971. The cast was as follows:

VIVIAN	Barbara Mitchell
MICK	John Hollis
CLAUDE	Clive Merrison

Produced by John Tydeman

VIVIAN.   Shall I tell you what what I bought today? Not
           enough enough oxygen in this block, why always
           headache. Spoke caretaker, caretaker says speak
           manager, manager says local authority local
           authority won't give us won't give us the money.
           Said I said what's the no point giving us faster –
           all be dead corpses in the faster lifts if there's
           not not not not not enough oxygen. Caretaker
           caretaker said his part his personal if it was up
           to if it was down to him would put big plants big
           plants plants plants in every room. Do stop
           walking about, Mick. Mick, do keep still as if you
           were paying as if you were hearing me.

MICK.   I'm waiting for my son.

VIVIAN.   Listen, it will take your mind take your mind
           off. What I said plants plants would take money.
           Earth plants earth would all have to come in
           from the park and the park the park authority
           the park authority wouldn't permit. Because
           hardly any park hardly any park left. My sister
           told me she went went went went to, four days
           four days days days to get and the crowd was
           the crowd was the crowd was just like home.

MICK.   How late will he be?

VIVIAN.   The grass can only – Mick why not go up on the
           roof and walk about walk about about in the
           haze? There's no room in this room in this
           room. You take five five steps remind that mad
           cat cat in cage at the zoo up and up and down
           up and –

           He sits down.

           Yes sit do sit and breathe quietly. Breathe
           quietly. It was Claude's own it was Claude said
           his own idea to come so he will. Shall we do
           some more of the big jig big jigsaw?

           MICK *pays no attention.*

           The grass. The grass in the park the grass can
           only be seen over the over the over the heads

heads of the crowd and fenced off so you can see see some because of course where the crowd walks where the crowd walks it's just mud. So what I bought what I bought was look an oxygen spray and spray spray oxygen in the room. (*She sprays it.*)

MICK.   Yes, spray it about. Let's have plenty of it. Don't spare. Claude will see his poor old dad knows how to live. He can give me all the money he likes and be sure I'll make good use of it. Not like his mother, who won't take a pound from him. Say nothing about her. But I know what money buys. I can enjoy a fortune.

VIVIAN.   I can I can too.

MICK.   Your husband earns.

VIVIAN.   Mick you know I only only I only live with him for the room. Where where else can I go where can I go if you won't won't have me in your room to live?

MICK.   It's too small for two.

VIVIAN.   All the rooms are the same are the same size.

MICK.   All too small.

VIVIAN.   But you know I feel nothing nothing I feel nothing for him only you.

MICK.   An old man.

VIVIAN.   Not not an old man.

MICK.   An old man.

VIVIAN.   Not very very.

MICK.   Not at all. Not old at all. When I was young there were men my age who did a day's work. I could work. My body is a bit out of use. But I can still touch my toes. My mind is a bit – my mind is not stretched. We must get some new puzzles. I am at an age where the things that go wrong with me won't get right again. But not much wrong. Claude will see quite a fine old man.

VIVIAN.   He'll be proud proud of his father.

MICK.   Proud? Do you think?

VIVIAN.   'I hope I'm as handsome handsome as you Dad
            when I'm as old as your age,' Claude Claude will
            say.

MICK.   He gets his looks from me. His mother had a
            certain brightness but not so much the shape of
            feature. You weren't born when I was his age so
            you missed all that happy time. I had fair hair,
            long fair hair, long was the thing then. But
            Claude's better looking than I was. The last time
            I saw him he sat in this chair. His mother stood
            there by the window. She'd brought him to say
            goodbye. He'd won a scholarship to his college
            in Africa. He was fourteen. His face – oh a
            brilliant child.

VIVIAN.   Did he look look like he looks when you see him
            see him sing?

MICK.   Sometimes when I see him in a programme –
            you'll laugh.

VIVIAN.   I never never laugh.

MICK.   If I'm alone sometimes I kiss him. That is to say
            I kneel down and put my mouth to the screen.
            Father and son counts even today. Then of
            course I find the picture has changed. I'm
            kissing an announcer or a tank. I feel a fool. But
            thousands of little girls must do the same.

VIVIAN.   When he comes shall I go shall I go out?

MICK.   Out? Out in the street?

VIVIAN.   Of course not out in the street in the street do
            you think I'm mad? Out of the room out out of
            the way, down in the down down in the lift to
            my room or the shops.

MICK.   Don't you want to meet him?

VIVIAN.   But it's five years since you haven't seen him for
            five years.

MICK.   He'll give you his autograph if I ask him.

VIVIAN.   You'll want to want to talk talk heart to not with
            a stranger not with me here.

MICK.   No. No no. You must stay. I haven't seen him
            for five years. You're still young. You can help
            us speak to each other.

VIVIAN.   I should like to be able to say I'd seen seen him
            spoken spoken to Claude Acton spoken to
            Claude Acton perhaps touched him.

MICK.   He'll like you. Who knows? There may be
            money for you. He's a sweet good kind boy. He
            has given money to strangers.

VIVIAN.   To me to me me do you think?

MICK.   If not never mind. He'll give me so much I can
            give you what you like. A daily dress. Eggs.
            Oxygen.

VIVIAN.   Mick, if you do do do get a cottage in the
            cottage in cottage in the park –

MICK.   Yes, I'm going to get a cottage.

VIVIAN.   Mick, I shall stay I shall stay with you because I
            want to get out get out of the Londons and not
            live in a tower tower tower block and you would
            have enough room you would you would have
            enough room for me there. And though you're
            in middle late late middle age I shall I shall I
            shall stay with you though I'm still young and
            look look younger than I am if you want if if if
            you want me if you want me.

MICK.   Yes, I'd like that. It's something isn't it to be
            happy at times and make someone happy. Let's
            stay together a long time shall we, because I like
            you.

VIVIAN.   I wish wish we could go go away now. I wish he
            would hurry hurry and get here. I'll look out
            and see if there's a car in the car in the jam. He
            must have a car a car licence to bring a car in

the Londons if anyone can afford it Claude
Acton.

MICK.   You look. I'm too shortsighted. I can't make out
the street.

VIVIAN *peers down at the street without opening the
window.*

VIVIAN.   Not not your eyes it's the fumes and fumes and
haze. I can hardly hardly – no no only buses
buses only buses hardly moving today. There's a
fire.

MICK.   Near?

VIVIAN.   No, do you see do you see black smoke far over
far over there?

MICK.   Those fanatics said they'd do something or other
today. Did you see on the news?

VIVIAN.   No, but what what kill themselves I suppose.

MICK.   Themselves or others.

VIVIAN.   At night night in the night I'm afraid I'm afraid
Mick I'm afraid if I wake in the night I think
the block the block is going to go up to go up in
flames any any any any moment go up in – ah!

MICK.   What? Is it him?

VIVIAN.   Look look.

MICK.   Where?

VIVIAN.   I think I think it was a bird it was a bird a bird
bird a bird.

MICK.   What? What?

VIVIAN.   Bird.

MICK.   A bird in the Londons?

VIVIAN.   Small brown brown I think it was a bird.

MICK.   A sparrow. A sparrow is a small brown bird. I
didn't see it.

VIVIAN.   Shall I open open open the window?

MICK.   No.

VIVIAN.   Yes yes yes you might see.

She opens the window. The distant roar of traffic.

MICK.   Shut it at once. The haze. The stink. Uh.

VIVIAN *shuts the window.*

Spray your oxygen about. You'll kill me.

VIVIAN.   (*spraying oxygen*). But the bird was a good a
            good-luck sign good luck for us, Mick.

MICK.   Claude can't have seen a sparrow. He's not
            twenty.

VIVIAN.   I remember I remember birds but bigger than
            that, it shows I'm not so young not so young as I
            – well I am thirty thirty had you thought? But
            what's youth youth youth these days? They don't
            enjoy enjoy any more and I can still I can still
            enjoy enjoy myself and you can you can.

MICK.   There were still some birds in the eighties.
            When I was a young man there were flocks of
            birds. What you remember is pigeons. Now they
            were a plague before elimination. They fouled
            the towers. I have honked the horn of my car in
            London streets at flocks of pigeons pecking at
            the bread thrown to them by some old woman
            dead now. And birds whose names you may
            have seen at the zoo, blackbird, starling, bluetit,
            I have seen them with my own eyes wild in the
            gardens of the Londons long ago.

The doorbell rings.

VIVIAN.   Mick Mick.

MICK.   He's come.

VIVIAN.   Mick press the press press the buzzer buzzer
            press the buzzer.

MICK.   (*into intercom*). Who is it? Claude?

A buzzy voice replies.
(MICK *presses the buzzer to open the downstairs door.*) Come up, come up.

VIVIAN.   Now at last the new fast some point at last in the new fast fast lift. He'll be here here at any in a moment at any moment he'll be he'll be here oh Mick he'll –

The doorbell rings.

MICK.   Open the door, Vivian.

VIVIAN.   Do I look look do I look all all right?

MICK.   Open the door.

VIVIAN.   (*opening the door*). Come in come come in.

CLAUDE *comes in unsteadily and stops.*

MICK.   Claude, my Claude, Claude. How tall you are. You haven't changed. Is it really you? (*He comes towards* CLAUDE.)

VIVIAN.   We've been waiting waiting –

MICK.   Do you feel all right? You look pale.

CLAUDE *collapses.*

VIVIAN.   Careful.

MICK.   He's falling.

VIVIAN.   Fainting he's fainting.

MICK.   Chair.

VIVIAN.   Here in the chair chair here here in the chair in the chair.

They sit him in a chair. Pause.

CLAUDE.   Be all right. Wait.

MICK.   Get some water.

VIVIAN *gets some.*

CLAUDE.   Just sit a minute.

MICK.   Claude, are you ill? What's happened? How can I get a doctor?

VIVIAN.   Here here you are, water here's some water.

MICK.   Have a sip of water, Claude. I've got the glass. There. There.

CLAUDE.   All right. Thank you. Better.

VIVIAN.   What what shall I do?

CLAUDE.   Nothing. All right. Thank you. Sorry. Didn't know how far how far it would be.

MICK.   How far?

VIVIAN.   In the traffic the traffic the jam.

MICK.   You're tired out by sitting so long in the car.

CLAUDE.   Walked.

VIVIAN.   Walked walked Mick he walked.

MICK.   Walked, Claude? Where from? Did the car break down?

VIVIAN.   Programme I saw programme said might be quicker to walk walk in the Londons than buses if only the air —

MICK.   Where is the car? Is it safe?

CLAUDE.   No car.

MICK.   But you have, Claude.

CLAUDE.   Did have.

MICK.   Was it stolen?

VIVIAN.   The crime rate the crime —

CLAUDE.   No no, got rid of it, I — got rid of it. Thought I'd like to walk. Do like. Just far.

MICK.   But to walk in the Londons. The air. The danger. You'll meet fanatics out in the open like that. They kill you. You must never do it again. What if you'd fainted in the street?

CLAUDE.   I'm here.

VIVIAN.   But someone famous famous like you to walk —

CLAUDE. Please don't.

VIVIAN. – walk in the Londons only fanatics and bad bad –

CLAUDE. Please.

MICK. Well it's lovely to see you, Claude.

VIVIAN. Let me spray some oxygen oxygen spray. Do you good and I feel I feel I need something I need something. (*She sprays oxygen.*)

CLAUDE. Wanted to see you. You're all right?

MICK. Oh yes. Yes. I make the best of what I can get. The little room is hard to bear because of course I remember the old days when people had more than one room. I don't get out of course. But I change the colour scheme from time to time. It's not a bad block. Large television. Lots of music. We complain about the air but the plumbing works. We've no sewage problem. There's no water of course but that's the same anywhere. I have books. I read. It passes time. And puzzles. All kinds of puzzle. Jigsaw, Chinese, mind tickles in the paper. Vivian and I do puzzles sometimes all day. We follow your movements when we can. You've been in China just now. It makes us feel less shut in.

CLAUDE. You hear from mother?

MICK. Hear from your mother? Now and then.

CLAUDE. She's gone off, hasn't she? Gave up all her gave up all her things. Not that she had much, she was never – Tried to give her – when I first earned – but she wouldn't. February she wrote me she'd formally relinquished her room, burnt her cards, just gone. So many do.

VIVIAN. Not many in the normal normal way only fanatics –

CLAUDE. That's what she is of course if you call them that.

MICK.   I never did understand your mother. She was
           always sad about one thing or another. I used to
           turn the news off, it upset her so much. Twenty
           years ago. The news is very much worse now
           and it must have turned her mind, poor woman.

VIVIAN.   It's a madness they say sweeping the country
           sweeping all the countries they say.

CLAUDE.   What about Alexander?

MICK.   Alexander? No, I'm out of touch.

VIVIAN.   Who? Alexander who? I don't know who
           Alexander –

CLAUDE.   My half-brother.

MICK.   Yes I have an older son, much older. By my first
           marriage, which I have just mentioned, I think.
           My first wife married again. She did well. A rich
           man. She flies. You may meet as you go about,
           do you Claude?

CLAUDE.   Once or twice.

MICK.   Tell me about her.

CLAUDE.   Very striking still from a distance. Armed guard
           always of course because stones are thrown. But
           laughing it off.

MICK.   Alexander doesn't keep in touch. He was always
           too full of ideals. His wife is a doctor too?

CLAUDE.   Do you not know then about the baby?

MICK.   They had a baby? Did they?

CLAUDE.   Wife wouldn't have another abortion though
           hadn't got exemption. They kept moving
           country to country to avoid the regulations.
           Born in Egypt I think.

MICK.   Boy or girl?

CLAUDE.   It died.

VIVIAN.   Oh no how sad how sad why did it die?

CLAUDE.   They killed it.

VIVIAN.   Why why why did they why?

CLAUDE.   They changed their minds. It cleared their conscience. It wasn't a licensed child.

MICK.   I would rather not have known about it, Claude.

CLAUDE.   I'd rather you did know about it.

VIVIAN.   Were they sent sent to prison were they sentenced to prison?

CLAUDE.   Five years for evading abortion but suspended since the child was dead. Gone as doctors to one of the epidemic areas now so no more to hear of them.

MICK.   Alexander was a pretty baby.

VIVIAN.   Babies are always always pretty and make you want want one if you see if you see a baby I want one but they shouldn't evade I've never dared never dared evade the regulations. But if I did if I did have if I did have one have a baby I couldn't I couldn't kill it more than kill myself I couldn't kill –

MICK.   With all his mother's money Alexander could have bought a licence.

CLAUDE.   Went in for the lottery. Thinks it's wrong to buy licences. So do I.

MICK.   You mean you'll go in for the lottery? With your money? What do you earn it for if you won't use it?

CLAUDE.   Won't have a child at all.

MICK.   You're young yet. Don't let's quarrel about it.

VIVIAN.   It's fanatic to kill a fanatic to kill a baby like killing yourself killing myself I'd never but fanatics do do do it hundred at a time I saw saw last night on the news a hundred hundred in a burning block some singing singing and some screaming and today today they say there are more more something going to happen. Life in the life in the Londons is no fun no no fun

these days and the sooner we go to the park go
to the park –

CLAUDE. Going to the park?

MICK. It's what I hope for.

CLAUDE. Live there?

MICK. It's all I want.

CLAUDE. Got money then?

MICK. Not yet.

CLAUDE. Be better off with my mother walking about.
Still open country some places. Risk is you starve
of course like most people. I've seen that. Given
what I can but five million pounds goes in a day.

VIVIAN. You've given given five million five five million
pounds?

CLAUDE. Yes.

VIVIAN. You're even richer than I thought richer than
how many millions many millions have you got
left?

CLAUDE. None.

MICK. Not so much as a million?

CLAUDE. Gave it away.

VIVIAN. All all gave it all?

CLAUDE. Yes.

MICK. All to strangers?

VIVIAN. But we watch we watch the news all the time to
see you and it never –

CLAUDE. Did it this morning. Got rid of all my things and
sent the telegram I was coming to see you.

VIVIAN. No oh no Mick Mick I'm frightened.

MICK. What about me, Claude?

CLAUDE. Wanted to see you.

MICK.　　You could have spared me half a million. A couple of hundred thousand. For your father.

CLAUDE.　You wanted money?

MICK.　　My cottage.

CLAUDE.　Didn't think of you. You're alive here.

MICK.　　You didn't think? You didn't think of me? Of course you did. Your father sitting here in his little box? I think of you all the time. You were one of the last children born in the Londons. People used to crowd round your pram because you were beautiful even then. What do you think a licence cost to have a second child? Can't you even pay that money back? How dare you give five million pounds away to strangers?

CLAUDE.　People do.

MICK.　　Oh I know that, it's the fashion isn't it? When I was young we had more sense.

VIVIAN.　Mick don't Mick don't make him angry.

MICK.　　Do you think no one was starving then? In the sixties, seventies, eighties? Do you think there weren't any wars when I was a young man? You're not the first person to see horrors. We learnt to watch them without feeling a thing. We could see pictures of starving children and still eat our dinner while we watched. That's what we need to survive. Your mother was no good at it so her mind went and she's gone off to die in a jungle gnawing a leaf or some nonsense. There's still meat in the Londons if you can pay. There's rations of food and water for each room. We can stay alive if we stay in the blocks. I told her that but she would go. She came to see me. She came at night. I was frightened when I heard the bell but I let her in. Do you know what she said? 'Come and let us end our lives together.' I was always fond of her. I said she could move back in here with me but she wouldn't do it. She would be off. She looked older than me. She said, 'Let me listen to some music and have a really good drink of water because I won't be able just to turn on music and water any more.' I turned on some music and gave her water with ice in it. 'I could almost stay,' she said. Then she got up and out she went without a word.

CLAUDE.   You should have gone.

VIVIAN.   Mick don't you see what he see what he is?

MICK.   I'm not saying I like it here. The rich get out. You could have got me out.

CLAUDE.   Half a million to put you in the park? You'd be better dead.

MICK.   What do you know about dying?

VIVIAN.   Mick stop stop Mick.

MICK.   I could talk about dying when I was young. Let go of me, Vivian. Now I'm going to die soon enough. I only need a little pleasure.

VIVIAN.   Mick don't you see see how he looks how he looks at you? Don't you see why why he's come he's a fanatic Mick come to kill us kill kill kill us come to kill us.

MICK.   Is she right?

VIVIAN.   I knew knew always knew fanatic fanatic would come and kill, always saying millions dying hunger dying war hunger war every day so we kill die kill too and shock shock into stopping but doesn't stop, saying die kill die leaving rooms blowing up blowing up blocks shooting self burning self shooting own family or strangers strangers in street on the news and I switch off I switch I switch off but now I can't and I'm glad glad no more waiting so do it kill me do kill me now and get it over over get it over.

CLAUDE.   I haven't come for that.

VIVIAN.   Not?

CLAUDE.   Not going to kill anyone else. Just came to see
           my father. Thought he'd be glad afterwards that
           he saw me once more first. Not happening till
           this evening so there's been the day to fill with
           last things. You've nothing to be frightened of.

MICK.   Claude, what stupid idea is this? I'm not angry
           about the money. You can always earn money.
           If you live to be as old as me you could earn all
           that money a hundred times over. You could
           give it away each time, what about that, and start
           again. That would do more good, wouldn't it?
           And in your life there would be happy times. In
           everyone's life. You would love someone almost
           certainly. Even without children, even with
           everything the way it is and getting worse you
           could be happy at times. There are always
           moments.

CLAUDE.   Better be going.

MICK.   Going? No, wait, let me make it clear.

CLAUDE.   (*getting up*.) Time I went.

MICK.   No, sit, stay there a moment. In the chair.

           CLAUDE *sits down*.

           Looking at me. Your mother's eyes. My hair. I
           had hair like that, Claude, but longer was the
           thing then.

CLAUDE.   (*getting up*). Easier if I go now. Goodbye.

MICK.   Wait.

CLAUDE.   What?

MICK.   Something I forgot to tell you. We saw a
           sparrow. Do you know what I mean? It's a bird.
           A sparrow.

CLAUDE.   Must have been nice for you.

MICK.   It was, it was. I wish you'd seen it.

CLAUDE.   Goodbye then.

MICK.   It must still be about somewhere. If you keep

your eyes open –

CLAUDE *goes.*

Claude, Claude, not like that, don't go, tell me when you'll come and see me.

VIVIAN. If we look look out of the window we may see him may see him going.

MICK. I can't see so far down.

VIVIAN. I'll open open the window.

MICK. Yes, yes, open it.

VIVIAN *opens the window.*

VIVIAN. Oh the smell.

MICK. Never mind, never mind, look out. Is that him? It's someone isn't it? Is it Claude? I can't see.

VIVIAN. The smoke hurts my eyes hurts – yes it's him.

MICK. There he goes then, there . . . I can't see him.

VIVIAN. Yes yes I can I can just just I can just see him still still just –

MICK. Still?

VIVIAN. No he's no no he's gone.

MICK. Shut the window. Spray your stuff about.

VIVIAN *shuts the window but stays looking out.*

VIVIAN. Look more look more flames.

MICK. Not from him?

VIVIAN. Not what not from him?

MICK. No, I'm sorry. What a silly mistake. I thought for a moment he was –

VIVIAN. No no no from a block a block another block on fire.

MICK. Spray the spray about. I've a headache again.

VIVIAN *sprays oxygen.*

VIVIAN.   Have a drink let's have a drink drink of water.

MICK.   Stupid boy.

VIVIAN pours a small glass of water each from the jug.

VIVIAN.   Though the park the park is mostly rows of cottages mud a little little grass if you like we could go this spring this spring we could go this spring to see see to see the grass and flowers flowers in the park.

MICK.   I'm too old.

VIVIAN.   No no not too not too old because I would come too I would come and it would be an adventure for us to go an adventure to go together and enjoy enjoy ourselves in the park.

MICK.   You'd better move your things into this room.

VIVIAN.   Yes I will I will and I'll get some new puzzles new harder harder puzzles for you though I can't do the sky on the big jigsaw with all those blue blue bits of sky – as if sky was blue – all look the same but you're so good at it. We can do that we can do that tonight and listen to music. We'll see news news of Claude on telly we'll see news of Claude.

MICK.   Yes I think his death might get a mention. Switch it on.

SCHREBER'S
NERVOUS ILLNESS

Author's Note

Schreber's Nervous Illness was based on *Memoirs of My Nervous Illness* by Daniel Paul Schreber, translated by Ida Macalpine and Richard A. Hunter and published by William Dawson & Sons Ltd in 1955 as Volume 1 of a Psychiatric Monograph Series.

Daniel Paul Schreber, a judge, spent ten years in asylums as a schizophrenic and wrote his memoirs there. What happened to Schreber after he left Sonnenstein is not certain. It is said that his family bought up most copies of his memoirs and destroyed them. There is some evidence that when his wife died, four years after his discharge, he was again admitted to an asylum and died there five years later.

Characters

SCHREBER, a judge
WEBER, a psychiatrist
JUDGE
GOD and RAYS

The voices of the rays are described by Schreber as 'soft lisping noises'. When God Ariman speaks it is a 'mighty bass'.

Time Schreber became ill in 1893 and was discharged in 1902

Place Asylums in Leipzig and Dresden.

Schreber's Nervous Illness was broadcast on BBC Radio 3 on 25 July 1972. The cast was as follows:

SCHREBER	Kenneth Haigh
WEBER	William Fox
JUDGE	John Ruddock
RAYS	Brian Haines
	Michael Kilgarriff
	John Sansom
	Sheila Grant

Produced by John Tydeman

Part One

SCHREBER. God was always in a precarious position. The human soul is contained in the nerves of the body. God is all nerve and his nerves turn into whatever he wishes to create. But although he enjoys what he has created he has to leave it to its own devices, and only rarely make contact with human nerves, because they have such an attraction for God's nerves that he might not be able to get free and would endanger his own existence.

My doctor, Professor Flechsig, had an ancestor who abused his power as a nerve specialist by keeping hold of some divine nerves and conspiring with them against the Schreber family, plotting to deny them children or a profession like nerve specialist which would bring them closer to God. Nerve contact was made with the Schrebers regardless of the danger to both God and the Schreber souls. Flechsig finally tried to commit soul murder, taking over another's mental powers. Soul murder has been attempted on me.

And so the Order of the World has been broken and God and I find ourselves in a situation that has never arisen before. His existence is now threatened by mine. For his nerves stream into my body against their will and cry continually in the sky for help.

'Nerve ray' music.

WEBER. The retired President of the Court of Appeal, Daniel Paul Schreber, Doctor of Law of Dresden, was admitted to this asylum at Sonnenstein of which I, Dr Weber, am the director, in 1894 and has been here ever since. It is not his first illness. Ten years earlier he was treated for a serious attack of hypochondria by Professor Flechsig.

SCHREBER. White lies may sometimes be indispensable to a
nerve specialist but were hardly appropriate in
my case, for Professor Flechsig must soon have
realised he was dealing with a human being of
high intellect. But I was eventually cured, and
therefore I had at the time no reason to be
other than most grateful to Professor Flechsig.
My wife worshipped him as the man who had
restored her husband to her, and kept his
picture on her desk for many years. After my
recovery we had quite a happy life despite the
repeated disappointment of our hope of being
blessed with children. I was nearly fifty and did
not like to think of the Schreber family tree
coming to an end with me. But in 1893 I had
the very great honour for one so comparatively
young to be appointed President to the Court of
Appeal at Dresden.

While waiting to take up office I occasionally
dreamt that my nervous illness had returned.
One morning while still in bed I had the highly
peculiar feeling that it really must be rather
pleasant to be a woman submitting to
intercourse. This idea was so foreign to my
whole nature that if I had been fully awake I
would have rejected it with indignation.

As President of the Court of Appeal I had to
preside over five judges as much as twenty years
senior to me and all at home with procedure
which was new to me. I was driven to achieve
their respect by unquestionable efficiency so that
I soon overtaxed myself mentally. By the time I
had mastered my office I was sleeping badly.
Again and again I was woken by a recurrent
crackling in the wall of our bedroom. Naturally
we thought of a mouse. But I now recognise
such noises as undoubted divine miracles. Right
from the beginning there was the intention to
prevent my sleep.

My illness began to assume a menacing character
to my wife and I travelled to Leipzig to see
Professor Flechsig. I was moved by his
eloquence when he spoke of the advances in

psychiatry since my first illness and gave me hope of curing me completely with one prolific sleep. But the sleeping-drug failed. During the night I got up in an attack of anxiety to make a kind of suicidal attempt with a towel, which woke my wife. Next morning Professor Flechsig took me to his asylum.

WEBER. At the beginning of his second stay at Professor Flechsig's clinic, President Schreber mentioned mostly hypochondriacal ideas and said he would soon die.

SCHREBER. I continued without sleep. I could not occupy myself in any way. Even jigsaw puzzles or patience increased my nervous tension so much that I had to stop. So I passed the days in endless melancholy, thinking almost exclusively of death.

My wife tried again and again to raise my spirits with plans for the future. I could only shake my head in disbelief. When she went away for a few days my condition deteriorated so much that I said I did not wish her to see me in such a low state and her visits ceased.

Then began the communication with supernatural powers, particularly the nerve contact Professor Flechsig kept up with me so that he spoke to my nerves without being present in person. I realised he had secret designs against me. I had begun to distrust him when I asked him if he really honestly believed I could be cured and he held out certain hopes but could no longer look me straight in the eye.

WEBER. Ideas of persecution soon appeared in the disease picture, based on hallucinations, which at first occurred sporadically but later ruled his whole thinking and feeling.

SCHREBER. Professor Flechsig and the divine nerve rays under his control forced me to think incessantly and denied me man's natural right to give his nerves a rest by sleeping or at least thinking nothing.

RAY.   What are you thinking of now?

SCHREBER. When my nerves did not reply the question was
           answered for me by the rays, falsifying my
           thoughts.

RAY.   What are you thinking of now?

RAY.   He should think about the Order of the World.

RAY.   Why do you not say it aloud?

RAY.   Because I am stupid perhaps.

SCHREBER. Though it was dangerous for God to approach
           living beings it was quite safe for him to draw
           the nerves of a corpse up to himself. They were
           then purified so that he could make use of
           them. They became part of him as the
           forecourts of heaven, protecting both the lower
           God, Ariman, and the upper God, Ormuzd,
           from contact with human nerves. The state of
           blessedness of male souls was incidentally
           superior to the female state, which was an
           uninterrupted feeling of voluptuousness. But
           now God's nerves were attracted away from him
           towards me so that all states of blessedness
           ceased. The souls which were not yet purified
           were also attracted, and soon Professor Flechsig
           was joined by hundreds if not thousands of dead
           souls.

RAYS.   (*many talking at once so that only occasional phrases
           are intelligible*).

           Flechsigs and Schrebers belong to the highest
           nobility of heaven.

           We expect a furtherance of Catholicism from
           your behaviour in Saxony and Leipzig.

           Two hundred and forty Benedictine monks.

           I am a Viennese nerve specialist called
           Startkiewicz, a baptised Jew, and I wish you to
           help me make Germany Slavic and institute the
           rule of Judaism. It is I, not Professor Flechsig,
           who should administer God's interest in his
           provinces.

We are members of the Students' Corps in Leipzig to which Professor Flechsig belongs as a drinking member and he has raised us all to blessedness.

Daniel Furchetegoot Flechsig lived towards the end of the eighteenth century and is now here as an assistant devil because of his part in a soul murder.

A turmoil of voices and ray music.

SCHREBER. Though God might destroy mankind if it threatened his existence, the Order of the World provides that one good man would always be spared and he would be unmanned so that he could bear children and repopulate the world. Twice the male genitals have withdrawn into my body and I have felt a quickening like the first sign of life of an embryo. Only the fact that as well as God's pure rays impure souls like Flechsig were present prevented the completion of the process in accordance with the Order of the World. The chosen survivor is looked after while nobody else exists by fleeting-improvised-men set down by miracle when they are needed. Since all the figures I saw at this time were not real people I did not feel inclined to speak to them.
Professor Flechsig knew about the unmanning. He laid a plot that my female body should not be used to repopulate the world but be handed over to someone for sexual misuse and left to rot. My medical treatment was designed to futher his plot. I was kept in bed for weeks and my clothes were removed to make me more amenable to female voluptuousness. I was given medicines for the same purpose which I spat out when the attendant poured them forcibly into my mouth.

RAY.   It is your duty to fight the attendants.

RAY.   That will show your manly courage.

RAY.   It is your duty to starve yourself to death.

RAY.   It is better to die than to be abused and forsaken.

RAY.   Why don't you drown yourself in the bath?

RAY.   Because I have no manly courage perhaps.

SCHREBER. I repeatedly put my head under water. Sometimes the attendants would pull up my feet for a joke or repeatedly duck my head and then force me to leave the bath.

It was natural for me to see my real enemy only in Professor Flechsig and to regard God as my ally. It was not until later that I realised that God must have known of the plan to commit soul murder on me and hand me over as a female harlot, if indeed it was not his idea. But though this may seem abominable the instinct of self-preservation can be roused in God as in anyone else, and it was only this that made him try to destroy me. The idea of morality can only arise within the Order of the World, the natural bond that holds God and man together. When that is broken, power alone counts. So neither on God's nor my part can there be a question of moral infringement.

My increasing nervousness attracted more and more souls, who lived in my head for a short time as little men and then dissolved in my body.

RAY.   I come from Cassiopeia.

RAY.   From Gemma.

RAY.   From the Firmament.

RAY.   I am the Lord of Hosts.

RAY.   The Good Shepherd.

RAY.   The Almighty.

SCHREBER. And they dripped from the sky onto my head as thousands of little men. Bad news came in from all sides.

Music plays through the following:

RAY.   Orion has been given up.

RAY.   Venus is flooded.

RAY.   The solar system will have to be disconnected.

RAY.   Only the Pleiades can be saved.

RAY.   The human race lasted fourteen thousand years but now it is lost.

RAY.   The earth has only two hundred years to go.

RAY.   It is over now.

The music stops.

SCHREBER. I was the last human being left. The figures of Flechsig, my attendants, the strange patients, were all fleeting-improvised-men. The starry sky seemed to be extinguished. I could not make sure as my bedroom window was closed up by a heavy shutter at night.

Music.

I was sitting in a railway carriage driving into the depths of the earth and into the past. First there were forests of leafy trees but as we went lower it became darker and blacker. I walked across a large cemetery where I crossed my own wife's grave. Sitting again in the vehicle I advanced only to point 3. Point 1, the earliest beginning of mankind, I dared not enter.

Music.

I was raised up to Blessedness. Below me the whole earth rested under a blue vault.

Music.

I frequently sat on the floor of my bedroom clad only in a shirt. My hands, which I set firmly on the floor behind my back were lifted up at times by black bears. If I looked through the peephole in my door I saw small yellow men whom I had to be ready to fight. Outside the window cats

with glowing eyes appeared in the trees of the
asylum garden.
It is understandable that I lived for years in
doubt as to whether I was really still on earth or
on some other celestial body. I thought I might
be on Phobos, a satellite of the planet Mars, and
wondered whether the moon, which I sometimes
saw in the sky was not Mars itself.
Professor Flechsig went away for the Easter
holidays. He kept calling himself 'God Flechsig'
so that his wife thought he was mad. He shot
himself in the police prison in Leipzig. I saw his
funeral procession. I realise now that this is not
what actually happened. But it is the divine
opinion of what should have happened to
Professor Flechsig. What is quite certain is that I
had Flechsig's whole soul in my body. It was a
fairly bulky ball thrown into my belly to perish,
but when it tried to get free I was moved by pity
and let it escape through my mouth. I
remember distinctly the foul taste and smell.
I was no longer kept in bed but walked regularly
in the garden. There were two suns in the sky.
The garden was in bloom.

RAY.   That is Flechsig's miracle.

SCHREBER. When I sat on a camp stool in the garden in a
black coat with a black flap hat I felt like a
marble guest who had returned from times long
past into a strange world.

WEBER.   The patient sat for hours completely immobile
in a hallucinatory stupor.

SCHREBER. I have since noticed with interest in Kraepelin's
textbook of psychiatry that many people whose
nerves were excited had been in contact with
supernatural voices accompanied by visual
hallucinations. But it seems psychologically
impossible that I suffer from hallucinations. The
hallucination of being in contact with God can
only develop in someone who already has faith
in God. But I was never a believer. My gift lay
in cool intellectual criticism rather than an

unbounded imagination. I had occupied myself
too much with the doctrine of evolution to
believe Christian teaching. So it is impossible
that what I have experienced should be
imagination. Psychiatry will have to recognise
that occasionally the phenomena may be
connected with real happenings and cannot be
brushed aside under the catchword
'hallucinations'.

**Part Two   Schreber is transferred to Dr Pierson's private
asylum, known to him as the Devil's Kitchen.**

SCHREBER. Early one morning, perhaps in June, three
attendants appeared in my cell with a suitcase
and told me I was leaving the asylum. Since they
were only fleeting-improvised-men I did not
think it worth asking where the journey was to
lead, and in any case I could not fare worse than
I had in Flechsig's asylum. I never saw him
again.
As soon as I arrived at the Devil's Kitchen I was
surrounded by fleeting-improvised-men.
Everyone in the asylum looked like someone I
knew. My special attendant was an attendant of
the Court of Appeal in Dresden. The chief
attendant was a young man called Mr von W
whom I had met at an east-coast resort.

RAY.   He has already led another life as the insurance
agent Marx on another planet.

SCHREBER. When I left Flechsig's asylum he drew up to
heaven some of von W's nerves so that he still
influenced me by influencing my attendant. I
was amused to see that though they were allied
against God they disliked each other. Von W
was so proud of his noble family that he would
hear no good of Flechsig, while Flechsig's pride
in his intellectual superiority made him regard
von W with contempt. Impure souls were

graded as Satans, Devils, Senior Devils and Basic Devils, and when they appeared as fleeting-improvised-men they were carrot red with a peculiar offensive odour. Von W had a red face and hands.

RAY.   Von W has given false evidence about you in a state enquiry.

RAY.   He accused you of masturbation.

RAY.   His punishment is to be your servant now.

RAY.   Flechsig should serve you as a charwoman.

RAY.   Why don't you box von W's ears?

RAY.   Because I have no manly courage perhaps.

SCHREBER.   And so I boxed his ears to be rid of the voices. I was let out into a pen, a desolate sand pit without bush or shrub, and nothing to sit on but two primitive benches. Into this pen were crammed forty or fifty people. In private asylums one usually finds only well-to-do patients but here there were extraordinary fellows in linen overalls covered with soot. Sometimes while I was looking at one he would suddenly run about with a different head. When the signal was given to come in they all crowded to the door but there would not have been enough room for them all in the asylum and I think some stayed outside and dissolved, since they were, after all, fleeting-improvised-men. Among them was a cousin of my wife's who had shot himself. He ran about continuously with a bundle of newspapers which he used as something soft to sit upon on the hard wooden benches.
              Now that the world had come to an end, an attempt was made on a distant star to create a new human race by using some of my nerves.

RAY.   Creation will only extend as far as the fishes.

RAY.   As far as the reptiles.

RAY.   As far as the lower mammals.

RAY.   There are new human beings out of Schreber's
            spirit.

RAY.   They are very small.

RAY.   They are quite cultured.

RAY.   They keep cattle proportionate to their size.

RAY.   Schreber is their national saint.

RAY.   Schreber has their God in his belly.

SCHREBER. I did indeed have this friendly soul in my belly.
            It had a peculiarly practical turn of mind, a
            fundamental trait of my own character, so that I
            recognised in him flesh of my flesh and blood of
            my blood.

**Part Three   The terrible miracles of the first year at
Sonnenstein and how Schreber's attitude changed.**

WEBER.   In June 1894, after two weeks at Dr Pierson's
            private asylum, the patient was transferred to
            the Country Asylum, Sonnenstein. He was at
            first completely inaccessible.

SCHREBER. I was still convinced I was not dealing with
            human beings so I kept mostly silent and I must
            leave open the possibility that I was right. One
            day I saw my wife enter my room and I was
            petrified for I knew she was dead. Her
            reappearance is an unsolved riddle to this day. I
            did not say very much to her as I thought she
            was fleetingly improvised for the occasion and
            would dissolve on the stairs.

WEBER.   This physically strong man lay or stood
            immobile, though with jerking of the facial
            muscles and tremor of the hands, and stared
            with frightened eyes into space. He refused
            nourishment so that he had to be forcibly fed
            and it was only with great difficulty that he was

gradually made to eat regularly again. He also retained his stool, apparently deliberately, so that he was at times incontinent.

SCHREBER. Even now the miracles I experience hourly would frighten any other person to death, but they are nothing in comparison to the miracles to my body during that first year at Sonnenstein. I had a worm in my lungs; my ribs were often smashed; or my chest was compressed so tightly that I could not breathe. My stomach disappeared altogether so that I could not eat. Sometimes von W would provide a stomach for me by miracle just before a meal, but often he changed his mind and suddenly took it away again so that food and drink were simply poured into my empty abdomen and ran down into my thighs. I gradually went ahead with eating without a stomach and grew quite calm about everything that happened. This may sound extremely strange but what can be more definite for a human being than what he has lived through and felt on his own body. Far more threatening were the miracles against my reason. Sometimes my skull was sawn apart in an attempt to pull the nerves out of my head. There were two little men in my feet, a little Flechsig and a little von W, who attempted to pump out my spinal cord, which next to the head was considered the seat of reason. One can imagine my apprehension as I saw it float out of my mouth in little clouds as I walked in the garden and I did not know whether my reason was vanishing into the air. The little men also interfered with my eyes because the rays' power is lessened if they see something, so they kept closing my eyelids. If I wiped them off my eyes with a sponge it was considered a crime against God's gift of miracles and the little men were at once set down afresh. Hundreds of little devils were assembled on my head looking for signs of its destruction. They had a horrible head compressing machine like a vice which was screwed up till my head was almost pear-shaped and of course gave me great pain. These severe miracles lasted only a few months but for some time my whole body was tormented. When walking I was forced to lie down, when I lay down I was chased off the bed. The rays did not seem to realise that a human being who actually exists must be somewhere. I had become an embarrassment for God in whatever position I might be.

One night the lower God, Ariman, spoke. I was lying in bed and I heard his voice outside the window. Anyone not hardened to terrifying miracles would have been shaken to the core. Even the impure souls were impressed and kept out of the way. He did not sound friendly.

GOD. You're a wretch, a wretch, and I will destroy you. You will soon feel my power and wrath, you wretch.

SCHREBER. Next day in the garden I saw the upper God, Ormuzd. It was the sun surrounded by a silver sea of rays, and it was so bright that I kept trying to look away but the attendant seemed quite indifferent to the sight. This showed conclusively that he was a fleeting-improvised-man for a real thinking human being would have found it of the highest interest.

My outward life was very monotonous during the first year at Sonnenstein. I mainly sat motionless the whole day on a chair at my table. Even in the garden I sat still.

RAY. Not the slightest movement.

RAY. It is your duty to keep absolutely still.

RAY. You must keep as still as a corpse.

SCHREBER. This foolish idea of the divine rays was based on God's not knowing how to treat a living human being since he usually dealt only with corpses. I considered immobility a duty to God, to free him from the embarrassment in which he found himself. I could attract more impure souls by lying still and, by destroying them in my body, give God more power in the sky. So I made the sacrifice of desisting from every movement for several months. I did not dare change my position in bed. I made this sacrifice for God since despite the evidence I could not get myself to believe that he harboured evil intent towards me. But the holiness of my purpose was so attractive to the divine rays that they could not forsake me. So one began to falsify my frame of mind through miracles to give the impression of a frivolous human being given only to the pleasure of the moment, whose attraction it was hoped would be less. At first I resisted the cursed creation of false feeling. But as time went by I allowed the influence. I found I really felt less unhappy in this way and I had to admit that all my efforts to help God had not achieved very much. I tried to live for the day and accept what life had to offer. I started smoking cigars again which I had not done for years. But even so the rays did not achieve their purpose. As with all miracles contrary to the Order of the World they had willed evil but created good. For they did not manage to weaken the attraction of my nerves but only made me feel less unhappy. And so a period of great suffering came to an end.

During that first year at Sonnenstein my physicians could not judge my behaviour correctly, assuming of course that they were human beings. They did not know I was fighting a sacred battle for the good of mankind and my appearance of a dullard brought many indignities as if they had forgotten my high official standing. My attendant frequently threw me back in the bath when I wanted to get out or woke me by pulling my beard. At meal-times he tied a napkin round my neck as though I were a child. Sometimes I resisted – when they wanted to remove the washbasin from my bedroom or take me to a cell fitted out for raving madmen. But this only led to senseless scenes of violence so later I kept silent and suffered.

I condone the excesses my attendant was guilty of in view of his low education, but I was always conscious of the deep wounds to my sense of honour.

Part Four   Schreber's life improves but he is still under attack.

Piano music.

WEBER.   In November the patient's stiff posture loosened a little. He became more mobile and started to speak coherently. Gradually his excitement mounted with loud laughter night and day and persistent hammering on the piano. In the garden he would stand for a long time staring into the sun and grimacing or bellowing loudly with threats and curses.

Or he raved in his room against soul murderer Flechsig, or shouted abuse out of his window at night so loudly that the townspeople gathered and complained. On the other hand he could now read and play chess and play the piano and was more amenable even in the middle of one of these noisy scenes, answering simple questions in a somewhat patronising way.

SCHREBER. My living conditions now became more bearable. A small piano was put into my room and it was a great help in drowning out the nonsensical twaddle talked by the rays, who of course tried to stop me playing. My fingers were paralysed, the direction of my gaze was changed so that I could not find the correct keys, even the piano itself was the object of miracles and the strings frequently broken. Superficial judgement might lead some to assume that I caused the strings to snap by senseless banging. This was my wife's repeatedly stated opinion.

But let anyone try to hit the keys as hard as he likes, even with a hammer or a log of wood, the keyboard may be broken to pieces but he will never break a string.

Though my outward life had improved there was still the attempt to unman me, not to renew the world but to degrade me, because it was thought that an unmanned body would lose its attraction for rays. My sexual organ was retracted, my moustache removed, and the lower God, Ariman, sometimes spoke.

GOD.   I wonder whether to make you somewhat smaller.

SCHREBER. My body indeed shrank about 6 cm, approximating the size of a female body.

RAY.   Is he not unmanned yet?

SCHREBER. I suppressed every feminine impulse. The female nerves that had penetrated my body in great masses could not gain any influence over my way of thinking, though I could not prevent when lying in bed a feeling of soul voluptuousness, well-being without real sexual excitement. At last God realised that unmanning me was not the way to free himself.

RAY.   Schreber is to be retained on the masculine side.

SCHREBER. But God's new plan came from another mistaken ideal. Day after day the rays heaped poison from corpses on my body, hoping to suffocate me and destroy my reason which God wrongly thought would weaken my attention. Sometimes I put my feet through the iron bars of the window at night to expose them to the cold rain, which diverted the rays' attention from my head, so that I felt perfectly well except for frozen feet. But the physicians fixed heavy wooden shutters on my window and locked them at night so that my bedroom was in total darkness. They probably had no idea how this affected me in my struggle to defend my reason. But it filled me with a deep and longlasting sense of bitterness. What harm could have come to me other than catching a cold? I could only see the physicians as tools of the rays. Through a total misunderstanding of human thinking it is believed that my thoughts can be exhausted by being written down and that God will then be able to withdraw. So everything I think and do is written in books by rays on distant stars. This, of course, is absurd because human thinking is inexhaustible. The system became a terrible mental torture especially when a thought occurred that had already been written down, which of course happened many times a day.

SCHREBER. Now I will wash.

RAY.   We have already got this.

               Piano music.

SCHREBER. This is beautiful music.

RAY.   We have already got this.

               The piano stops.

SCHREBER. I had better go to bed.

RAY.   We have already got this. We have already got this.

               SCHREBER *shouts to drown out the voices.*

Part Five   Schreber accepts that he is turning into a woman and the miracles become less harmful

WEBER.   The patient was frequently found in his room half undressed. He declared he had feminine breasts, and he had his moustache removed.

SCHREBER. It was a beautiful autumn with a heavy morning mist on the Elve. The signs that I was changing into a woman became so marked that I could not ignore them. First my hands and arms changed, then my legs, bosom and buttocks. My male sexual organ was only prevented from disappearing by my resolutely setting my will against it. But after a few days observation of my body the direction of my will changed completely. I could see that the Order of the World demanded my unmanning whether I liked it or not and it was common sense to reconcile myself to becoming a woman. This would clearly lead to fertilisation by divine rays to create new human beings.

RAY. Are you not ashamed in front of your wife?

RAY. Fancy the President of the Court of Appeal letting himself be fucked.

SCHREBER. But I did not let the rays divert me from my purpose. I would like to meet the man who, faced with the choice of becoming a lunatic or a spirited woman, would not choose the latter. I still love my wife as much as ever but it must be hard for her to retain her love and admiration for me when she learns that I am preoccupied with changing into a woman. I can deplore the situation but cannot change it. I must guard against false sentimentality.

My new attitude caused a change in celestial conditions. If the rays found voluptuousness in my body it was an adequate substitute for the heavenly blessedness they had lost.

Now the voluptuousness was so great that some rays began to like entering my body. I considered it my right and duty to cultivate feelings of voluptuousness. Few people have been brought up according to such strict moral principles as I or practised such moderation in matters of sex. But to attract the rays I must imagine myself as man and woman in one person having intercourse with myself – it has nothing whatever to do with masturbation. God demands constant enjoyment, which is the

normal state for souls within the Order of the
World, and since he cannot escape from my
nerves it is my duty to provide him with it. If I
can get a little sexual pleasure in the process it
seems a small compensation for my years of
suffering.

Ariman was the first to enjoy entering my body
and he broke off his relations with Flechsig.
Flechsig's soul, which still had a good deal of
human intelligence, at once made an alliance
against me with Ormuzd. Ariman's miracles
became more harmless now and the voices more
nonsensical and so easier to bear as they fitted in
better with the right of a man to think nothing.

RAY.   David and Solomon.

RAY.   Salad and radishes.

RAY.   Little heaps of flour.

SCHREBER. Sometimes there were phrases which showed
            that God was not so devoid of understanding as
            he sometimes appeared. There was the thought
            that the policy of destroying my reason had
            failed.

RAY.   Knowledge can never be lost.

RAY.   Sleep must come.

RAY.   Permanent successes are on the side of the
            human being.

SCHREBER. Sometimes there was even an admission of
            guilt.

RAY.   If only I had not put you among the fleeting-
            improvised-men.

RAY.   What will become of me?

SCHREBER. Even God was aware of a thoroughly
            mismanaged affair.
            Through his complete failure to understand
            human beings God thinks that if no thoughts
            are formulated in words the person is
            demented. Sometimes he came close enough to

realise he is dealing with a human being of unimpaired mental powers. But he seems unable to learn from the experience. For as soon as I think nothing he thinks my reason is destroyed and he can withdraw. I am made to bellow to give the impression of someone bellowing because he is demented. But finally God realises that my power of attraction is undiminished, which causes great anxiety to those of God's nerves that are separated from the mass that managed to withdraw and they cry out woefully.

RAY.   Help help help.

RAY.   If only the cursed cries for help would stop.

SCHREBER.   Constant thinking is impossible; it is also impossible to spend the whole day in a state of voluptuousness. The art of conducting my life in the mad position I find myself, the absurd relationship between myself and God, is to find a fitting middle course.
Religious peoples must be perplexed that God can be surpassed mentally and morally by a human being. But my superiority is only relative. I know myself and I know other souls, while God does not know the human being and does not need to know him. His concern is the creation and evolution of the world and I acknowledge his eternal wisdom in his own field. As well as changing his attitude to me, God changed towards the impure souls, who had become such a nuisance that he made a raid among them and reduced their numbers. Von W's soul sat in my mouth or eyes for about a year and we exchanged some amusing ideas till it gradually faded away. I suddenly realised after not thinking about it for some time that it had vanished and played the funeral march from Beethoven's 'Eroica' in honour of its departing. Flechsig's soul remains but it long ago lost its intelligence and can hardly even enjoy the heavenly existence it unlawfully achieved. For nothing can exist permanently which is

against the Order of the World.

Though I now spent my time peacefully reading or playing chess and almost entirely avoided violence for two and a half years I did not sleep in my own room but in the padded cells for demented people. It is possible I sometimes spoke aloud at night. I was forced to make a noise to drown the senseless twaddle of the voices. I spent several hours of almost every night pounding with my fist against the closed shutters or groping in the dark cell and by miracles being made to hit my head against the ceiling rather than remain in bed when I could not sleep. No other patient had to stay in these cells more than a few weeks. I was kept there for two and a half years, long after the reasons for the measure no longer existed, through inertia on the part of the physicians. I do not wish to be acrimonious but my sufferings there were unbearable. How could I convince God that I existed when there was nothing in the cell but an iron bedstead, a bedpan and some bedding, and no light? Sometimes for hours on end I tied knots in the corners of my handkerchief, counted aloud particularly in French, repeated all the Russian departments and so on. And I suffered all this for two and a half years because human beings did not understand supernatural matters.

Part Six   Schreber decides that other people exist and shows how everything they do is caused by miracles.

SCHREBER. I took part in the Christmas festivities of Dr Weber's family and this and other incidents early in 1896 led me to a critical examination of my ideas about fleeting-improvised-men. I also began to read the newspapers and could no longer doubt that a real race of human beings existed. How could this be reconciled with my

previous experience? This difficulty is insoluble
by human beings since I am certain that my
previous experiences did not originate in my
head.

WEBER.   A change was noticed in the patient. He entered
into a lively correspondence with his relatives
and it must be admitted that the letters hardly
showed anything pathological but rather a
certain insight. The insulting laughing and
shouting continued so that the nightly isolation
had to be maintained but his occupations
became more various and continuous. He was
still little inclined to serious conversation and
soon started to grimace and utter short
interjections.

SCHREBER. Every word spoken near me is accompanied by
a painful blow directed at my head. The sounds
are caused by miracles and intended to interrupt
my feelings of voluptuousness and enable God
to withdraw. So at the slightest sound such as
opening the lock on my door, pressing the latch,
the entry of the attendant, I experience a pain
like a pulling inside my head as soon as God
withdraws tearing off part of the bony substance
of my skull.
I have incontestable proof that everything said
around me is caused by miracles. The rays that
God sent loaded with poison to destroy my
reason have appeared for years as talking birds.
If anybody says words similar to their set
phrases they become confused and cannot resist
my attraction. Each part of God wants to hold
back from me and push the other forward, so
the upper God makes people say words that
belong to the birds of the lower God, and vice
versa. At dinner Dr Weber keeps using words
from the birds' material so often that it is
beyond possibility of coincidence.
The birds incidentally are different according to
the season of the year. In spring they are
finches, in summer swallows, in winter sparrows
or crows. Of these species of fast-flying, singing

birds I have never seen one that did not speak.
But the pigeons in the asylum yard do not
speak, nor do the chickens, geese and ducks I
have seen on excursions from the asylum. I
would be most interested to observe bird life in
other parts of the country.
The rays continue their miracles against me but
they are becoming weaker. They begin sentences
which used to be complete when they had more
thoughts of their own but now I must complete
them.

RAY. Now I shall –

SCHREBER. – resign myself to becoming stupid. It is hard
to give a picture of the mental torture I suffered
through being irresistibly compelled to finish
every phrase the rays began. Gradually,
however, I accustomed my nerves to ignoring
them by simply repeating what the rays had
said, and so turning them into not-thinking-any-
thing thoughts.

RAY. Why because I –

SCHREBER. Why because I why because I why because I
why because I
Another unbearable change is that the voices
have slowed down.

RAY. W-w-w-h-h-h-y-y-y d-d-d-o-o-o etc. (Why do you
not shit?)

SCHREBER. This would cause great impatience to someone
not, like myself, inventive in using more and
more methods of defence. My main defence is
playing the piano; at night I recite poetry
silently – Schiller or Strewelpeter, the value of
the poetry does not matter. Even obscene
rhymes are valuable compared to the terrible
nonsense I otherwise have to listen to. When I
have silenced the voices God sometimes starts
the bellowing miracle till I am too breathless to
recite so I have to keep changing systems.
Counting up to a high number is a great help
but very boring. The last remedy against

persistent bellowing is swearing aloud, but I
hope this will become less necessary in future.
I must explain the question, 'Why do you not
shit?' God's complete lack of knowledge of the
human being makes him think that to shit is the
final act and that when I empty my bowels the
goal of destroying my reason is reached. But
whenever the need to defecate is produced by
miracle some other person is sent to the
lavatory. This I have observed so regularly that
one can exclude any thought of it being
coincidence.

RAY.   (*slowly*). Why then do you not shit?

RAY.   Because I am stupid perhaps.

SCHREBER. It really is fantastic nonsense that God in his
blindness and lack of knowledge of human
nature goes so far that he assumes a human
being who cannot shit for sheer stupidity. I find
now that I can manage best when I sit on a
bucket in front of the piano and play till I can
empty my bowels.
Though most of the miracles I have described
are damaging this is only because the Order of
the World is out of joint. But now that it has
been forced to draw near the world by the
attraction of my nerves, neglecting the rest of
the universe and suspending the state of
blessedness, the rays cannot fulfil their normal
tasks and have turned to performing useless
miracles, such as creating insects.
God can create only within the conditions he has
established so that wasps and bees appear on
warm days, gnats and moths in the evening. I
can predict without fail that as soon as I sit on a
bench in the garden, a fly, wasp or a whole
swarm of gnats will be created by God to
prevent my sleeping.
Miracles are directed against me and all objects I
use; miracles make people speak, cough, sneeze,
make horses neigh and dogs bark. But all this
activity contrary to the Order of the World is to

no purpose as human beings and animals can do these things anyhow and insects exist already in vast numbers. The miracles are at best a senseless game, at worst a torment. Even for God the situation is fraught with evils. His joy over newly created things soon gives way to anxiety and his nerves still come down to me with cries for help.

Ray music.

One might wonder whether I exaggerate or suffer from self-deception. But I have always been known for absolute truthfulness and more than usually keen powers of observation. The time will come when other human beings will have to recognise that my body has been the centre of divine miracles.

Everything that happens now is in relation to me. People may be tempted to think I am pathologically conceited. I know this very tendency to relate everything to oneself is common among mental patients. But in my case it is from God's point of view that I have become the human being round whom everything turns.

Because the patients are mostly madmen of low education, vulgar words are often uttered in the garden of the asylum which the rays want me to relate to myself. This used to end in scenes of violence, in which incidentally I always had the satisfaction of knocking my attacker to the ground despite violent miracles being enacted on my kneecap to make fighting impossible for me. So I now spend most of the time in the garden playing chess to maintain peace, even during the bitterly cold winter when I have to play standing up. When I play chess there is a rest from the stupid twaddle of the voices. They talk such nonsense that for a long time I doubted if God could be responsible for them, but it is just another example of his extraordinary ignorance. God can no longer claim infallibility since he entered into a

relationship with me contrary to the Order of
the World. It was he himself who devised the
whole policy against me. For a full year I was
concerned for my reason. But all attempts at
unmanning me for sexual abuse and destroying
my reason have failed. The Order of the World
does not provide even God with means of
destroying a human being's reason. So from this
apparently unequal struggle between a weak
human being and God I emerge despite my
bitter sufferings triumphant because the Order
of the World is on my side.

**Part Seven   Schreber decides to work for his discharge
from the asylum.**

SCHREBER. The constant nuisance caused by the lunatics
has made me decide to work for my discharge
from the asylum. I really belong among
educated people, not madmen. Although I have
a nervous illness I do not suffer in any way from
a mental illness which would allow my detention
against my will. So when I discovered that I had
been placed under temporary tutelage soon
after my admission to Sonnenstein I approached
the authorities for a decision as to whether the
tutelage was to be made permanent or
rescinded.

WEBER.   The patient has shown a recent change of
attitude. Whereas previously, perhaps because of
a more marked feeling of being ill, he was
resigned to his fate, he now energetically
demands the lifting of his tutelage, and expects
to return home. Whether President Schreber is
to be considered deprived of his reason in terms
of the law by virtue of his paranoia is for the
court to decide.

SCHREBER. The result of my approach to the authorities
was that a formal order for my tutelage was

made in 1900 based on a report by Dr Weber.
So I brought an action against the prosecuting
authority to have my tutelage rescinded.

WEBER.   I have delayed making a further report about
President Schreber's mental state because his
condition has not undergone a marked change.
If evidence is demanded of actual events which
would prove he is incapable of managing his
affairs, it is obviously very difficult in the case of
a patient who has been interned in an asylum
for many years. Although he has recently taken
meals at my table and joined in excursions to
Dresden, convincing results one way or the
other have not been obtained. Whatever we
discussed at dinner such as law, politics or
literature, he showed keen interest and correct
judgement. Sometimes, however, he will stare
rigidly, grimace and clear his throat. It required
his greatest energy not to utter bellowing noises
and while he was on his way to his room one
could hear his inarticulate sounds. During a visit
to his wife he could not repress the noises at
table so that a sign had to be given to the
servant girl not to take any notice.
He lapses still in prolonged attacks of bellowing
which will improve and he thinks he could avoid
disturbing his neighbours by living in a house
with a large garden. But in his morbid egoism
he does not consider how his wife would suffer.
Whether the patient would live within his means
is not certain. His striving for scientific
recognition of his ideas might lead him into
great expense. He still has no insight into the
pathological nature of his ideas and seeks to
have his memoirs published, of course without
success. It is incomprehensible that a man
otherwise of fine feeling could propose an action
which would compromise him so severely in the
eyes of the public were not his whole attitude to
life pathological. The memoirs themselves afford
the judge the necessary basis for a judgement as
to whether the mental illness is sufficient to
prevent the patient looking after his affairs.

SCHREBER. In 1902 the order for my tutelage was
confirmed. My last hope of having it rescinded
was the Court of Appeal at Dresden of which I
was formerly president. I made the appeal
myself in the following terms:
I do not deny that my nervous system has for a
number of years been in a pathological state.
But I absolutely deny that I am mentally ill or
ever have been. I do not wish to offend Dr
Weber but I must express my conviction of the
error of his report. It starts from the assumption
that everything that has arisen between God and
myself rests on pathological imaginings. I know
Dr Weber could only apply the standards of
common scientific experience. But the certainty
of my knowledge of God towers high above all
human science.
The question whether the voices I hear are
caused only by a pathological disturbance of my
nerves or whether some external being speaks to
me is simply one assertion versus another. I
cannot prove the miracles but only wish people
to recognise their possibility and hesitate to
dismiss the whole affair as nonsense . . .

Fade out and in.

. . . It remains to discuss whether this assumed
mental illness makes me incapable of looking
after my affairs. The onus of proof lies with my
opponent, the public prosecutor. In the last year
I have gone out unaccompanied and nobody has
noticed the slightest unreasonable behaviour.
The only thing that could be considered
unreasonable is that I was seen standing in front
of the mirror with ribbons and cheap necklaces
on my body. This only happens when I am
alone, never if I can help it in front of other
people. I have very good reasons for this
behaviour; at worst it can be considered a
harmless whim. The small acquisitions cost only
a few pence so do not come under consideration
from a financial point of view. They are bought
only to create a certain impression on God and

for this almost valueless articles suffice.
Naturally I would spare my wife any painful
sight. I showed her my adornments only with
some reluctance when out of forgivable feminine
inquisitiveness she insisted upon it. Naturally I
would not expect her to live with me if it should
be unbearable for her because of continued
attacks of bellowing. Dr Weber misjudges me
when he speaks of my pathological egoism and
claims I do not give a thought to my wife's
suffering. If any nuisance should arise from the
bellowing I would return to a closed institution
of my own free will.
I do not belong to the class of mental patients
who constantly insist on their discharge without
giving a thought to their future life. My life in
the asylum is not so unbearable that I should
prefer a lonely life outside. Should it prove
impossible I would return. But I must insist that
my stay in the asylum is a measure to which I
give my free assent as a human being capable of
looking after his own affairs.

WEBER. To be asked by the Court of Appeal to give
another report on Professor Schreber is a task
little congenial to me. I have been his doctor for
many years, for a long time he has been my
daily guest at meals, the relationship between us
is a friendly one. I sincerely wish that he may at
last obtain some enjoyment in life. But I am
asked to make a report which may question his
tutelage and deprive him of further happiness.
The free discussion of a patient's symptoms is
always a touchy matter for the patient. He will
never agree with the doctor unless he could
judge his condition correctly, which would show
he was not ill. I would have welcomed it if
another expert had been called.
The patient says in his appeal that my previous
report assumes his ideas are pathological. But it
is not an assumption. I can trace in the history
of his illness how the hallucinations gradually
developed till at last his system of ideas was
formed. His legal representative makes the point

that many people believe in miracles without anyone declaring them mentally ill; but the patient's belief is not the ordinary naive belief in miracles but was contrary to his earlier beliefs and grew out of his illness. It cannot be expected that the patient will see that the hallucinatory events are entirely subjective. He tries to show that his hallucinations are special and to find a basis of reality for them. But this is done by every hallucinating person. Otherwise he would not be suffering from hallucinations. The patient asks for a medical opinion about the development of his body. He cannot be induced to give up his belief in female nerves of voluptuousness, which he supposes to be found all over the body, particularly the bosom, although the female breast owes its form to milk glands and fat.

The patient is now allowed out unaccompanied and his conduct is never incorrect though he cannot avoid being conspicuous. Unless his control of the bellowing improves he will certainly be a disturbance at home. I am very sorry to have hurt his feelings by referring to his pathological egoism. I only meant that he underestimates his effect on other people. Married life would require considerable self-denial on the part of his wife. The court will know best how to judge these deviations from the normal. I would like to stress that they concern relatively unimportant fields. Apprehension for the future need not weigh as heavily now as previously.

JUDGE.   Judgement of the Appeal Court of Dresden in the case of Daniel Schreber, doctor of law, President of the Appeal Court retired, now residing in the Country Asylum, Sonnenstein, versus the Public Prosecutor re contesting the order placing plaintiff under tutelage.
The Court has no doubt that the plaintiff is insane. What to objective observation is hallucination is for him irrefutable certainty. But it is not sufficient grounds for placing the

plaintiff under tutelage that his mental processes are pathologically disturbed. It is necessary to establish that he is incapable of managing his affairs. The burden of proof rests with him who requests the order for tutelage.

One observation forced upon the judge was that President Schreber's intellectual powers had in no way suffered by his illness. The capacity to think logically is not however a sign of the ability to judge correctly all practical matters. But the plaintiff's movements outside the asylum have not given rise to any trouble worth mentioning and he has dealt with the money allowed him in an orderly fashion. He has not wasted money on his belief in miracles. The money he spends on female adornments is insignificant. Much greater sums are spent on whims by healthy people.

It is said the marital bond with his wife is threatened by his release. But for years he has lived apart from his wife so how could the relationship be worsened? Whether he will improve it by living with her is uncertain. One would have to try and see. But this has no bearing on his tutelage which must be for the well-being of the person concerned and not to protect the feelings of others.

It only remains that the plaintiff might compromise himself by the publication of his memoirs. But one considers him mad in any case. The Court of Appeal therefore believes that the plaintiff is capable of dealing with the demands of life whose orderly regulation is the object of the law. The tutelage inflicted on the plaintiff is rescinded.

SCHREBER. I am shortly to be discharged from the asylum. I naturally wonder about my future. For a long time I have expected to turn into a woman, but whether, in the conditions contrary to the Order of the World, it can be accomplished I dare not predict. It is possible that despite strong indications of femaleness I shall die a man. Being released from the asylum is no compensation for the suffering of the past seven

years. Some magnificent satisfaction must be in
store for me. While still in Flechsig's asylum I
coined the phrase 'There must be an equalising
justice'. Now I am beginning to have some idea
of my reward. Every day there are times when I
float in voluptuousness. An indescribable feeling
of well-being pervades my body. It is not
necessarily connected with sexual matters. When
reading a poem or hearing music or enjoying
nature in the country, I experience a foretaste
of blessedness. It is shortlived. At the height of
voluptuousness, headache or toothache is
produced by miracle. Sometimes I enjoy
voluptuousness up to my neck while my head is
in a bad way. But in the future voluptuousness
will prevail and I will enjoy in my lifetime the
blessedness granted to other human beings only
after death.

I hope that I shall not die in an asylum but at
home surrounded by loving relatives. There will
probably be some extraordinary phenomena at
my deathbed so I hope men of science will
attend. The question arises as to what will
become of God when I am dead. I think his
conflict with the Order of the World will end
and the impure souls will be completely
repressed, which so far he has not had the will-
power to carry through. He would then resume
his normal functions and renew the state of
blessedness, to which I would at once be raised
in view of my special relationship with him.
Throughout our relationship he has been ruled
entirely by egoism, and treated me with cruelty
and disregard as a beast does its prey. This may
confuse religious people as God cannot be the
ideal being of absolute love and morality that
most religions imagine. But it does not detract
from his grandeur, as normally no being would
exist detrimental to God's interest so that the
question of his egoism would not arise. His
hostility is at last losing its virulence and the
struggle against me may soon end. Meanwhile it
is a matter of making life as bearable as possible

for both parties.

The whole development appears as a glorious triumph for the Order of the World in which I can ascribe to myself a modest part. To the Order of the World I can only apply the beautiful saying that 'All legitimate interests are in harmony'.

As for my life at present, the miracles are more and more harmless, though I still suffer from tearing headaches which come and go with every withdrawal of rays. Though I welcome feeling incomparably better I realise that the less the miracles appear the less hope I have of convincing people of their reality, so my improvement gives me mixed feelings, as my only purpose in life now is to give man a truer insight into the nature of God.

The voices have slowed down so much that their hissing is like the sound of sand trickling through an hourglass. I can distinguish individual words only with difficulty. Naturally I do not bother, but try to ignore what is spoken. As soon as I have silenced the voices, I hear the talking birds, but what they say is immaterial to me. I am no longer hurt when the birds I feed cry out.

RAY. Are you not ashamed in front of your wife?

SCHREBER. Bellowing does not occur provided I count, but it is not easy to count for hours so sometimes I get out of bed and carry on some occupation to show I am a thinking person. In public places I can prevent bellowing almost completely by counting though I may have to make some little noise like coughing or yawning somewhat ill-manneredly. But while going for walks along country roads or in the fields I make things easy for myself and simply let the bellowing happen. Sometimes it continues for five or ten minutes, during which time I feel perfectly well. Anyone who saw me would, however, hardly understand what I was doing, and might really think he was seeing a madman.

THE HOSPITAL
AT THE TIME OF
THE REVOLUTION

Author's Note

The play is partly based on Chapter 5 of *The Wretched of the Earth* (*Les Damnés de la terre*) by Frantz Fanon, and also owes a lot to the writings of R.D. Laing.

Fanon was born in 1925 in Martinique. He studied medicine in France and was appointed head of the psychiatric department of the Blida-Joinville Hospital, Algeria, in 1953. He began helping the rebels and in 1956 resigned from the hospital to work for the FLN, and wrote *L'An V de la Révolution Algerienne* and *Les Damnés de la terre*. He died of leukaemia in 1961, a year before Algerian independence.

Characters

FANON
MONSIEUR
MADAME
FRANÇOISE
YOUNG DOCTOR
THREE PATIENTS (A, B and C)
MALE NURSE
POLICE INSPECTOR

FANON is black and about 30. He is head of the psychiatric department at the Blida-Joinville Hospital in Algeria. He wears white.

MONSIEUR and MADAME are middle-aged Europeans. FRANÇOISE, their daughter, is 17. She is neatly and prettily dressed in a style rather too young.

The YOUNG DOCTOR is an open-faced European in his twenties. He wears white.

The THREE PATIENTS are Algerians, wearing white hospital pyjamas.
A is about 30, slight, with bandaged wrists, depressed.
B is 50, a small man with a mole on his cheek, a peasant. He is in a stupor and if he reacts to anything it is with terror.
C is in his mid-twenties, very light skinned, excited.

The NURSE wears white.

The POLICE INSPECTOR is a large European of about 35.

The TIME of the play is during the Algerian war, about 1956.
The PLACE is the hospital at Blida-Joinville, Algeria.

There is no scenery except bare white walls, minimum of furniture: white upright chairs for most scenes; white beds for patients. Bright light.

FANON, MONSIEUR, MADAME *and* FRANÇOISE.

MONSIEUR. What a time for her to be ill. When all my
energies should be devoted – anything could
flare up in my absence. I have to keep my
fingers perpetually – Still this shouldn't take
long to arrange. But what a time to choose. As if
we hadn't enough problems.

MADAME. This is Françoise, our daughter, I'm afraid.
We've brought her to you because we can't stand
her any more. It was the advice of our own
doctor who said it would be the best thing for
her.

MONSIEUR. You have his letter on the subject?

MADAME. We're beside ourselves.

FANON. Yes I have his letter here. Françoise, could you
tell me what seems to be the matter?

MADAME. I don't think she'll be able to speak to you.
Come along now, sweetheart, sit up and speak to
the doctor. You make me really ashamed.
Because she's not like this at all, Doctor. She's a
very polite and very intelligent girl. The way
she's behaving now is all part of the trouble.

MONSIEUR. We haven't got all day to sit here.

FANON. Françoise?

FRANÇOISE. I am dying.

MADAME. You mustn't say things like that or people will
believe you.

FANON. Why are you dying?

MONSIEUR. You don't seem to understand, Doctor, there's
nothing at all wrong with her health. We've had
her given a thorough going over by our own
doctor. He's a very high-calibre physician as I'm

sure you know and naturally no expense has been spared in the way of blood tests, X-rays, cardiograms – I couldn't have done a more complete job myself and I'm a man who finishes what he starts, that is well known. And in his words she is physically a perfect specimen. No, she's perfectly fit. That's why we've brought her to you.

MADAME. Except that she's underweight.

MONSIEUR. That's because she doesn't eat.

MADAME. She can't be in perfect health if she's underweight, if I may just be allowed to speak. Nobody wants to be fat but it's not attractive to be underweight and she's always been very pretty up till now.

MONSIEUR. But we know why she's underweight. She refuses to eat. No one's suggesting we should forcibly feed her I hope. The point I am making is that there is nothing the matter with her body. Her system functions admirably.

FANON. Do you feel ill, Françoise? What do you feel is wrong?

MADAME. Are you going to answer the Doctor nicely Françoise or shall Mummy do it?

MONSIEUR. You won't get her to say what's going on.

MADAME. Speak up.

MONSIEUR. You want to keep it dark now don't you my pet? It's nothing to be proud of is it?

MADAME. My husband gets angry and I would of course because the things she does are enough to make the most long-suffering mother annoyed but I tell myself again and again, 'do remember she's not herself, she's not herself', and so I keep control of my temper and really feel sorry for her.

MONSIEUR. Will you speak! I've got work to do. The whole country could rise up while we sit here waiting

for Miss to think what she thinks she might feel,
and would she care if my whole world – It is
half past!

FANON.   Perhaps you could give me some idea of what's
been happening.

MONSIEUR. She's – we – she – you can see for yourself. It's
not for me to say she's mad, that's what we've
come to you for. It's a painful subject for my
wife, you realise, I hope. One doesn't put
seventeen years into rearing a child for this kind
of return. You're waiting for an example? Really
I try to forget, not to drag these sordid – last
week, one must after all face the facts, last week
she threw, she deliberately threw – an accident is
out of the question – she threw a cup of hot,
boiling hot coffee at her mother. It came very
near to hitting her and I don't have to explain
to a doctor what the consequences of that would
have been in the way of burns. It was black
coffee, you understand. As it was the cup was
broken, the carpet and wallpaper were stained
and though of course that's of no importance
yet it is a constant reminder as well as an
eyesore and a source of great anguish to us
both. None of this was perhaps so hurtful and
shocking as the language. You wouldn't think
to see her sitting there that she had ever
let herself hear any such expressions. That a
father should have to say all this. The only
possible explanation is that she didn't know what
she was doing. But what was worse and a really
decisive sign of illness she said more than once,
there is no mistake, I'm sorry, that she hated her
mother. So you can judge for yourself.

MADAME.   There are children who behave like that. You
mustn't think us too other worldly. But
Françoise has always been perfectly good. Until
this terrible illness attacked her she never gave
us an unhappy moment.

MONSIEUR. Oh it's not a case of a juvenile delinquent. I
abominate anything of that kind. I could never

bring up a child like that. In my capacity as a civil servant I administer a large area comprising both urban and rural elements so you see I know what I'm talking about. The native children are naturally born violent and dishonest and you even get European boys who are rotten through and through and that is something the law exists to deal with. The police and magistrates are locked in an endless struggle to curb and suppress and pacify – I know where I am there and I believe in the triumph of justice. But this is my daughter we're talking about. Part of me. The situation cannot have arisen. How can I make myself clear? My friends have often said to me, what a treasure you've got there. How happy she must make you. And she did. And surely she still could.

MADAME.   I've never understood women who complain about their babies. You know, 'He cried all night, he keeps wetting himself.' It never occurred to me to complain. Right from when I was a little girl with my dolls back in France I knew I should love being a mother and when I met my husband who was on leave in France at the time and he brought me here, everything was so different, the heat and light and the hatred, I've never been able to get used to the heat, but once I had the baby it was all just as I knew it would be, and she never cried at night, she was clean at a year, she was quick and clever at walking and talking and never got dirty, and people used to say, How do you do it? but I didn't have to do anything, it just never occurred to Françoise to be anything I didn't want, it simply didn't arise. If I think of her at three or eight or thirteen it's just the same, always pretty and smiling and liking to be with her mummy and daddy and what made us happy. At the most terrible times she always kept us happy.

FANON.   Terrible times?

MADAME.   I don't mean of course terrible times, I mean little ups and downs such as people have.

MONSIEUR. So what's your excuse then for making us suffer? I haven't heard you apologise yet. What do you think you're doing to your mother? Look at her. She never looked her age while you behaved yourself and now look at her eyes. When do you think she last had a night's sleep? You must stay here in hospital till you're better. Because I can't have her home in her present condition, it's more than anyone should be asked to bear. Home should be a refuge. She is not capable of home life and hospital would be in her best interest. Because this is a difficult time for everyone but Françoise has experienced none of it. Nothing at all. Her quiet nice life goes on as if it were somewhere else. She takes it all, her school, her dresses, her little bird in a cage, everything we do to protect that perfect life she is lucky enough to lead. And does she ever say thank you?

MADAME.   Oh it's not Françoise to be ungrateful. She knows your hard work is all for her. All the difficult things you have to do are only done to make this country a place where she can be happy. Think how she used to fling her arms round your neck when you came home and take her feet off the floor. She's always been very close to her father. I mean as a father and daughter often are. And close to me too. Very close indeed to her father and to her mother. I can always buy her clothes and know just what she likes. And if she doesn't greet you the same way now it's only her illness. Just as she put her dress in the dustbin. So it might be better if she came here just till she's herself again. It's very quiet and away from it all here. And almost cool. Françoise and I have always felt the heat. There are such delightful trees in the hospital garden.

MONSIEUR. Perhaps I should not do my duty. Perhaps I

should not serve my country. Perhaps I should not send her to a good school but should let her roam the streets all day. As she has done. Have we told you that? Augh. Do you see how I'm shaking? I'm quite exhausted. Do you see what she's done? She sits there so quietly but that's deliberate to make us suffer too. That girl has destroyed a happy family.

MADAME.   When she's better she'll be able to say how sorry she is. We'll be able to forget all about it.

MONSIEUR. If you don't mind me asking, Doctor, where are you from?

FANON.   Martinique.

MADAME.   That must be a nice carefree place. You must miss the singing and dancing. I saw a film once. In colour.

MONSIEUR. Yes, that's all right. I thought you couldn't be from here. The natives here, you'll have noticed yourself, they're not the sort of people to be psychiatrists. It's one more thing we have to do for them and we do it damn well too like everything else and what thanks do we get? I suppose you studied in France did you? In Paris?

FANON.   Yes.

MADAME.   Yes I noticed your accent was very good. You must find it terribly dull here if you're used to Paris. I've been there myself.

MONSIEUR. That's all right then. Just so we know where we are.

FANON.   When would you say the trouble began?

MADAME.   The whole catastrophe, Doctor, is due entirely in my opinion – I know I'm not a doctor in any way but I am her mother and I'm certain it's what she would say herself if she was well enough to discuss it – it's all due to studying too hard. Because her great aim in life, her one ambition is to go to university in Lyons. That's where I come from you see.

FRANÇOISE. Her one ambition is to go to university in
Lyons. That's where I come from you see.

MADAME.   So her aunty and uncle could keep an eye on her.

FRANÇOISE. So her aunty and uncle could keep an eye on
her.

MADAME.   And then she'd be out of danger.

FRANÇOISE. And then she'd be out of danger.

MADAME.   And could come back when the country is
pacified and back to normal again.

FRANÇOISE. And could come back when the country is
pacified and back to normal again.

MADAME.   Stop it.

FRANÇOISE. Stop it.

MONSIEUR. Pull yourself together at once Françoise, or –

FRANÇOISE. Shall I tell you why I'm dying? Because
someone wants to kill me. I won't say who just
now because sound goes through walls and into
people's minds. No, no, no, no, no. Don't switch
me off. She works perfectly well. She's Françoise
now, do you see? It's not a bad child at all. It's
just like a child.

MONSIEUR. Do you need any more? It's perfectly clear. I
don't know why I'm sitting here when important
investigations are under way which need my
constant surveillance. In the national interest, I
must be off. You can lock her up now as far as
I'm concerned. The child is mad. There's
nothing to discuss. She's broken my heart and
her mother's, which may give her some pleasure,
I don't know. I shall grieve for my little girl as if
she were dead. Because this person can't be my
child.

MADAME.   She'll get better, she's sorry, aren't you
Françoise? That's what she's trying to say. Look,
she's better, now.

FRANÇOISE. She's sorry, she's sorry. Hold me tight, don't let me get away. Hold me, hold me, hold me.

MADAME. Hush now, there now, hush. Mummy's precious. What will the doctor think of you? Hush now baby. Be a big girl.

FANON. You were saying you thought she had been studying too hard.

MADAME. Yes, because that's not the way to pass exams is it, to study day and night? I used to say to her, go and have fun, go and be with your friends, it will be far more help to you than sitting over your books all the time. And then – and this was the first sign of her illness – she started to complain that I was making her study, making her work all the time. And I said, No it's not true, you're the one that wants to work all the time, I'm saying you should go out and do what you like because that way you'll do even better in the exams because your head won't be so muddled. But she wouldn't go. She just cried and said we wouldn't let her do anything but work, we wouldn't let her live, and she simply wouldn't come away from her desk. There were girls we knew about, friends of hers, who were going out every evening in the most shocking way. But Françoise just would not relax no matter how much I told her she ought to.

FANON. Before that, did she have much social life?

MONSIEUR. None at all.

MADAME. Plenty.

MONSIEUR. She's far too young to take any interest in young men. That would have come later.

MADAME. I mean with her girlfriends from school. She was very popular indeed. No, she's never had a boyfriend, if that's what you mean. That hasn't arisen. She liked having her schoolfriends round and they would shut themselves up in her room and talk and talk as girls do. I don't know what about and I'd never ask because of course I could be sure it was nothing wrong.

FRANÇOISE. I have got a boyfriend.

MADAME. Françoise, you have not. She gets confused. I'm
sure she doesn't mean to tell lies.

FRANÇOISE. His name is Armand.

MONSIEUR. I thought it was clearly understood we'd heard
the last of him.

MADAME. Françoise, you didn't even like him.

FANON. Who is Armand?

MONSIEUR. It has no possible relevance.

MADAME. He was just a young man Françoise once met,
the brother of a girl at her school whom she
didn't really know. He was a student and had all
sorts of misguided ideas about making
concessions to the terrorists, he was no sort of
person at all, and it's very lucky we didn't know
him. I said to him more than once, 'You are a
guest and we do not discuss politics in this
house.' He was extremely rude to my husband.

FRANÇOISE. He liked me.

MADAME. No he didn't, Françoise, he was only after one
thing and when he found you weren't that sort
of girl he quickly went elsewhere. He knew I
knew what he was up to. If I'd left you alone
together for one minute I know what would
have happened.

FRANÇOISE. We were often alone and he never –

MADAME. You were never alone because he knew I was
keeping an eye on things. No, he had no interest
in you. I blame him very much for trifling with
your feelings.

FANON. What did you feel, Françoise, when you didn't
see him any more?

MADAME. She was relieved because she'd never liked him.

FRANÇOISE. I thought I did like him.

MADAME. No, he tried to persuade you that you did but
you didn't really.

FRANÇOISE. He was very rude to Daddy.

MADAME.   Yes, he was and I don't know why we're wasting time polluting our minds with the thought of him. He had far too good an opinion of himself as if every woman he saw was attracted to him. I know that look in the eye –

MONSIEUR. Can we get on? Can we get on or shall I go?

MADAME.   I think I was saying how Françoise studied too hard.

MONSIEUR. That didn't last long, did it?

MADAME.   I'm coming to that, don't rush me so much.

FRANÇOISE. I think of him when I touch myself at night.

FANON.   I'm sorry, I didn't quite hear –

MADAME.   None of us heard that and none of us want to.

FRANÇOISE. I think of Armand when I touch myself at night.

MADAME.   No you don't, Françoise. That couldn't possibly happen. You wouldn't want to do that. You can't tell me of a single occasion when it's happened. Can you? No, you see, it obviously never happens at all. Françoise is completely innocent as I was myself at that age and she doesn't know what she's saying.

MONSIEUR. Listen to me. One day the headmistress rang up my wife and asked why Françoise was not at school. She had in fact been taken to school as usual.

MADAME.   Not at school! My heart literally stopped beating. Naturally I thought she had been killed.

MONSIEUR. She hadn't been to school for a whole week.

MADAME.   She'd been slipping out as soon as my back was turned. My head swam, I had to sit down, I nearly fainted away.

MONSIEUR. We still haven't got out of her where she went or what she did. I no longer want to know. If

you can make her tell you I can trust you to
inform me of the details. You have my
telephone number.

MADAME.   I know something terrible happened to her,
didn't it, Françoise? She won't admit it. I don't
mean – that, the doctor made sure she was still –
you know, but it's not the only fate worse than
death these days.

MONSIEUR. Françoise has never set foot outside alone nor
ever wanted to because she's mature enough to
understand why not. She can't possibly have
looked after herself. It defeats me how she can
have shown so little consideration for her
mother.

MADAME.   Only last week a young woman who's a great
friend of a great friend of mine was in a café
when a bomb was thrown and her face has been
entirely disfigured so that no one will be able to
look at her. Luckily the woman who threw the
bomb misjudged in some way and was killed
herself. I don't know why a woman can do
anything violent. It is not in a woman's nature.
But the Arab women are so deceitful, far worse
than the men in my opinion. I hardly like to
have domestic help though I'm kindness itself
and always give them a little piece of cake if we
have any victories to celebrate. But you can't
trust them to play their part. Because I'm the
first to insist they give up the veil and be
educated. I'm a great believer in progress and
many of their customs are quite degrading so
how else can they be properly French? They
must wear proper clothes. But the very same
women who most stubbornly refused to improve
themselves and insisted on keeping their own
ways, these are the ones who dress like us now
just so they can come out of the native quarter
without being noticed and come into the shops
and cafés looking just like young Frenchwomen
and murder us. You can't tell who people are.
You can't tell where it's safe to step. I don't

know how Françoise is still alive, it's more than she deserves. How can I possibly sleep when we live in such danger?

MONSIEUR. My wife exaggerates the disturbances.

MADAME. I know of course they're only temporary.

MONSIEUR. There is no war and no revolution.

MADAME. I never suggested –

MONSIEUR. Except for isolated incidents the whole thing is completely under control. Particularly in my own area. And indeed everywhere. I'm not saying I don't have to be constantly on the alert to spot trouble before it can start. But I do, so that the danger is minimal, in fact in our area there's none at all.

MADAME. I was only saying Françoise should have gone to school.

MONSIEUR. The violence is committed by criminals. It is not part of any revolution. The majority of the natives look to us to protect them and restore order. And it is only the French who can pacify the land. Because the Algerian naturally has criminal tendencies. But thanks to the large number of arrests in the area we are in control. Out of danger. Entirely in control of the situation.

MADAME. Françoise should stay at school when we take her to school.

MONSIEUR. Of course she should. Otherwise the whole thing gets completely out of control. Anything could happen. What shocks me most, Doctor, is the deception. Anyone who's a member of our family is scrupulously truthful and honest and Françoise knows that. In the civil service for instance it's well known opportunities occur but I've never made an extra penny and no daughter of mine tells a lie.

MADAME. Françoise never told lies when she was little like some children we knew.

MONSIEUR. I only had to take her by the shoulders and look into her eyes and say, Françoise, Daddy knows, and she always told the absolute truth. And now –

FRANÇOISE. I don't think –

MADAME. What? Can't you go on?

MONSIEUR. She's forgotten what she was going to say and in any case it's rude to interrupt.

MADAME. And now to come home as if she was coming home from school and shut herself up in her room as if she was working and not to work at all. What was she doing in there? What was going on in her mind? Not that we want to know what goes on in her mind but naturally her parents have an interest. Perhaps you can get it out of her, Doctor, because we've tried and tried.

MONSIEUR. We know the kind of thing she was thinking. The things she sometimes comes out with that show you beyond any doubt. Because I must be off.

FANON. What things do you mean?

MONSIEUR. The poison and other nonsense.

FANON. The poison?

MADAME. When she started going to school again – I used to take her right into the classroom so we'd be quite sure, I'd see her actually sitting at her desk and be sure the teacher had seen her there, I would sort of wave at the teacher and point to Françoise behind her back so as not to attract attention and embarrass her – so there she was, quite good again as we thought, and the headmistress took me aside and said, Is Françoise ill because she's not working, she's not talking and she's not eating her dinner. That was another very nasty shock because of course she's never been finicky, she's always eaten everything on her plate. I don't mean she was

greedy either. She would never ask for more but
she'd eat up everything she was given. You
could use her plate again. Not that I would. So
when we asked her why she wasn't eating, what
do you think she said?

FRANÇOISE. It was true. We don't tell lies. The food was
poisoned.

MADAME.   There you are, you see. The food was poisoned.

FRANÇOISE. It was true. It was killing me.

MADAME.   But the other girls ate their dinner.

FRANÇOISE. The poison was only put in mine because it's
only me that's got to be killed. Do you know
what? When I left food on my plate at school it
was thrown straight into the dustbin. No one
else would eat it because they knew it was
poison. They sent it straight off to be burned so
no one would find out.

MADAME.   But Françoise, all the leftovers would be thrown –

FRANÇOISE. Do you want to kill me?

MADAME.   All the leftovers would be thrown in the dustbin
and taken to be burned. That's what they do
with rubbish.

FRANÇOISE. She wants to kill me too. All my life she's been
trying to poison me. It started in the milk when
I was a baby. She puts just a little in everything I
eat –

MADAME.   Who do you think is going to believe –

MONSIEUR. No, give her the rope.

FRANÇOISE. Just a little so there's no taste and she thinks I
won't notice. All my life, three meals a day,
think how much poison there is in me now.
Because it doesn't come out when you go to the
toilet. That kind of poison stays in and piles up
inside you till all your stomach and liver and
veins and nerves and head are full of poison
and then you die. But she hasn't killed me yet.

I'm not quite full. But if I eat one more meal in her house then the poison will reach the fatal amount – because I study biology at school, I know how the body works, you see – and then I'll be all poison and dead at last.

MONSIEUR. You see, you see? Now what are you waiting for?

MADAME. She pretends she's stopped eating altogether but what she does is she goes into the kitchen at some odd time and gets something for herself, never the right thing for the time of day and often not things that are good for her at all but spoonsfuls of sugar, just sugar, and I've always given her well-balanced meals to have just the right effect on her bowels and her teeth and her complexion and her figure. The dangers of living in a climate like this can be counteracted by a proper diet. Or she'll come down in the night and eat the very food she refused at dinner-time and I catch her out then, I say to her, well it wasn't poisoned, was it, darling? But of course she won't admit she's had anything. She won't say a word. But instead of giving her a good smack I cook all her favourite foods to try and make her eat something because she's lost –

FRANÇOISE. She cooks all her favourite foods. Why? To make her eat. Why? To poison her. Why? She wants to kill her. Why? She hates her. Why? Why does she hate her? She's not a bad child to be killed and poisoned and shut up and beaten like that.

MONSIEUR. I'm delighted you can see for yourself what we have to put up with.

FRANÇOISE. They're after me now. They'll have me in a minute. Let me tell you first because you must protect me. Because I've been to the police but they won't help me because they work with my father and he stands by them whatever they do so they stand by him. My mother has killed a little girl. But no one punishes her, do they? My father has killed far more people. I can't give you a list of the names but I hear the screams all night.

MONSIEUR. I think we've had enough of this filth.

MADAME.   She sleeps perfectly soundly but she does sometimes have bad dreams, don't you Françoise, and you call out sometimes for Mummy and I come in and give you a drink of water.

FRANÇOISE. I hear screams all night. I don't know how to hear the screams. I think I'm screaming myself.

MADAME.   That's right, it's all your horrid dreams, the screams are all in your head.

FRANÇOISE. The screams come through the walls into my head. Is Daddy cross? I'm being beaten. Don't be cross. Francie's a good girl now.

MADAME.   Of course he's not cross. He's never cross. He's only cross if Francie's a bad girl. Daddy loves Francie and Mummy, and Mummy –

FRANÇOISE. What does he do, fuck you with a bottle? Pump soapy water up your arse? I can keep my mouth shut. I know who he loves and who he kills and who he's going to kill now. But you can't kill me because I was never born. There's no girl of that name here. You can do what you like but she won't speak.

MADAME.   I just can't listen to such language. It makes me feel quite ill.

MONSIEUR. Take her out of my sight, Doctor. Please take her away.

FANON.   I should like in any case to give her a physical examination and some tests. Will you come this way, Françoise? Will you go with the nurse?

FANON *shows* FRANÇOISE *out, then comes back himself.*

MONSIEUR. I don't feel at all well myself. I get pains in my
stomach. But naturally her illness gets all the
attention.

MADAME.   You shouldn't let her speak. She gets herself
over-excited.

MONSIEUR. You couldn't give me something while I'm
here, Doctor, for my stomach?

FANON.   You should go to your own doctor for that.

MONSIEUR. There's no time. There's never a moment.

MADAME.   He works too hard. Often he's up all night.
Sometimes I ask myself what it's all for? In my
weak moments. I even think I wouldn't refuse to
leave the country. Not really of course.

MONSIEUR. The country needs us. It's the country of my
birth. I'm ruining my health in the service of my
country and I'm proud to do it. That's why we
can't keep going if Françoise is like this.

MADAME.   I get so worried I hardly know what to think.
Though of course you're right.

MONSIEUR. You won't find an area that has been so
thoroughly cleared of subversive elements. And
there were a great many misguided
sympathisers. We help them to see their mistake.
And most of the people I'm happy to say are
very grateful. They just want to live in peace.
And so do we all. But meanwhile of course I
lose sleep. I need to be present at the
interrogations to get the information first hand.

MADAME.   How happy we'll be when order is restored.

FANON.   Does Françoise know about the interrogations?

MADAME.   She's not at all interested in politics.

FANON.   Where do they take place?

MONSIEUR. Sometimes at the police station, sometimes in
the empty wing of our house because numbers
have sometimes been a problem. Yes I bring my
work home with me.

MADAME.   He doesn't spare himself.

FANON.   Are you kept awake at night?

MADAME.   No, because I haven't slept well for a long time.
My doctor prescribes a very efficient sleeping
pill so I sleep perfectly now, thank you.

FANON.   And Françoise?

MADAME.   She wouldn't need sleeping pills because I don't
believe in them for children and she has always
slept perfectly well.

FANON.   She doesn't hear screams?

MADAME.   She has nightmares sometimes which are part of
her illness. No Françoise's life has gone on just
as if it were peacetime. If anyone suffers I think
it's her parents. There are no screams in any
case.

MONSIEUR. I can't understand why you speak as if it were
wartime. You do it again and again. The
outbursts are very few and far between. But I
hope you see, Doctor, that we can't have
Françoise at home in our present condition. You
are keeping her in hospital.

FANON.   The hospital is very crowded and there is a
waiting list except for emergencies. I'm afraid I
can't say until I see the result of the tests.

MONSIEUR. But I'm not having her at home.

FANON.   If you could wait in the waiting-room. I will go
and see Françoise now.

FANON *goes.*

MONSIEUR. She must not come home. Why didn't you
make that clear?

MADAME.   Whatever do you think he's doing to her? I
hope he's gentle. She'll be so frightened of a
Negro.

MONSIEUR. I'm not waiting. I'm going back to work. I can't
trust anyone else to be in control. You'd better

come too. He's perfectly civilised, he was
educated in Paris.

MADAME. Hadn't I better wait?

MONSIEUR. You're not to bring her home.

MADAME. I can only do what the doctor says.

MONSIEUR. This is a matter of your loyalty. She is not
coming home until she's better.

MADAME. He's certain to keep her here because she's mad.
I'll just wait to make sure he does. He'll have all
the proper equipment. It will be so much nicer
for her. It's very clean and the trees are so
shady. Poor Françoise. Now she's not here I do
love her.

They go out.

2

FANON *and the* YOUNG DOCTOR.

DOCTOR. When I saw the policeman outside I wondered
which of us he was after. I thought they'd found
out who's been pinching syringes and surgical
dressings. But it seems he's brought a prisoner.

FANON. Yes, we've been asked to make a report on him.

DOCTOR. Grim-looking chap.

FANON. The prisoner?

DOCTOR. Both of them. But really anyone stealing
hospital supplies is asking for it.

FANON. You're likely to be caught.

DOCTOR. I mean once you start helping them where do
you stop? Every one of them whose life you save
goes straight off and starts killing. You might as

well be a terrorist yourself. It's different if they come to hospital. I wish they would. Once they're here they're our job and the rights and wrongs don't enter in.

FANON (*looking at papers*). The prisoner is a fifteen-year-old boy who has killed three people.

DOCTOR. Don't tell me. He stabbed them ten times each.

FANON. His friend and his friend's mother and sister.

DOCTOR. I'm not saying I'm glad to think of them dying up in the hills with no medicine. It doesn't bear thinking about but nothing does these days so that doesn't get us very far. But they are the enemy after all. They'd kill me, although I'm a doctor. And you.

FANON. The boy hasn't been in trouble before. He was an average pupil at the village school, his teacher says here, and not particularly difficult.

DOCTOR. I won't mention names but I do have my suspicions of a certain nurse. She seems to me unusually tender with the native patients. I could be wrong. What do you think?

FANON. I think we should think about the prisoner.

DOCTOR. But it gives me a funny feeling that someone I work with – after all, what if they drove us out? It's not a selfish viewpoint. I'm thinking for instance of my father. His land really is his land. He's devoted his life to it. He's as much a father to his workers as he is to me. And a lazy ungrateful lot of children they are. But one has to put up with that and not expect too much and slowly help them to be more like us. Who would look after them if we were gone?

FANON (*reading*). 'The incident took place when a few olives were picked from a tree on the land of the accused's father by the boy's friend. He took out a knife and stabbed him repeatedly.'

DOCTOR. The remarkable disproportion between cause and effect is typical of the Algerian crime of violence. It's what Professor Porot says about the Algerians being born criminals.

FANON. 'The victim's mother came out of the house screaming, and he stabbed her too.'

DOCTOR. The explanation is in the structure of the brain. Professor Sutter explains it very clearly. The Algerian has virtually no cortex. He is dominated by the lower part of the brain just like the lower vertebrates and quite differently from Man as we know him, European Man, who is distinguished from other creatures by cortical thinking. We use the frontal lobes and Africans don't. Don't you agree there's no need to enquire further?

FANON. 'The victim's sister ran up and was also stabbed repeatedly, the mutilation continuing after she was dead.'

DOCTOR. You must know the work of Doctor Carruthers of the World Health Organisation. He says that since the African doesn't use his frontal lobes it is just as if they had been removed so that the African is like a lobotomised European. It accounts for the impulsive aggression, the laziness, the shallowness of emotional effect, the inability to grasp a whole concept – the African character. It's no wonder they behave as they do if that's what they're like. I don't know why we have to waste our time making a report. A European might have to be mad to behave like this but it's just what we should expect of an Algerian.

FANON. 'The accused then went home and washed and waited calmly till he was arrested. He showed no emotion and his only statement was "Well, he took the olives".'

DOCTOR. There you are. They're never really responsible for their actions in our sense of the word.

FANON. Shall we go and see the patient now?

DOCTOR. You didn't take anything personally did you?

After all, it is what they teach in medical school in Algiers and it's common knowledge even if you don't agree. I certainly don't think of you as any different from me. No one would know you weren't white except to look at you. No one would think you didn't use your frontal lobes.

FANON *goes out during the last speech, and the* DOCTOR *follows talking.*

3

Three hospital beds in a row with three Algerian PATIENTS, A, B *and* C.

Dinner is brought in by a MALE NURSE *who goes out again. A and C eat; B doesn't react at all.*

C.   Someone is always saying I'm a coward but I hope I have proved to his satisfaction that it is not the case and someone else is the coward I think I am. Is that clear?

A.   No one's saying you're a coward.

C.   I shut myself away for love of my work.

A.   Yes, I liked my work.

C.   Because I've never been interested in politics, only in engineering, and there's nothing wrong with that. You wouldn't say I was a European would you? I've a pale skin but that's from being ill and indoors so much. You wouldn't say I was a European? To look at me you'd see I was an Algerian, wouldn't you, just by looking at me.

A.   I can hardly remember any more that I was a draughtsman. I'm not a draughtsman.

C.   Are you saying I'm a European?

A.   No.

C.   Because in the street people used to say I was a
      coward and a traitor. If I went into shops they
      wouldn't serve me. Everyone looked at me on
      the bus, I had to jump off before it stopped. So
      I stayed in my room and I looked in the mirror
      and there was a European looking out, so I
      broke the mirror, which settled him. I couldn't
      come out of my room to eat with my family
      because they were wondering why I was still
      with them, and why I hadn't gone to join the
      Maquis like other people's children.

      The NURSE *comes back and encourages* B *to eat.*

NURSE.   Come on now, what about some dinner? Here
         we are.

B.   No no no no no no no.

      He throws himself about, held by the NURSE; *at last
      he quietens down.*
      The NURSE *takes his plate away.*

C.   He thinks he's the only one who's been tortured.
      I've been tortured. I'm an Algerian patriot,
      that's why, they knew me when they saw me.
      They arrested me straight away. I was beaten. I
      can show you the marks but they're nearly
      healed up now. What are those bandages? Were
      you tortured too?

A.   No.

C.   I was. What have you got bandages on for? Are
      you pretending you were tortured?

A.   I cut my wrists. I've told you that before. Don't
      you remember anything we say to each other?

C.   Of course I do.

A.   What do you know about me?

C.   You've got a wife.

A.   When she came to see me yesterday I hadn't
      seen her for more than a year. She didn't ask
      me any questions. When we lived together it was

hard when I used to come and go without
telling her why, because since being married
we'd come to love each other and we used to
talk. She was very young and she'd been one of
a big family so she depended on me for not
being lonely. But she got over that. If I was
away all night she never complained or asked
where I'd been. So she never knew what I did.
Though when I couldn't sleep she lay awake too.

C.   Are you saying you were working for the
        revolution? Are you calling me a coward, is that
        what it is? I did braver things than you've ever
        done. Have you ever walked up to an armed
        soldier and taken his gun away? Have you?

A.   No.

C.   I did that. When the voices got too loud in my
        room because the people outside had a secret
        network of amplifiers so they could keep up a
        constant accusation that I was a coward, a
        traitor, a European, I ran out of my room to go
        and show them. I expect you had weapons,
        didn't you? I expect someone gave you a
        weapon? Did you ever have a weapon?

A.   Yes.

C.   No one gave me a weapon, did they? How was I
        expected to fight for my country? What was the
        good of calling me a coward and not giving me
        a weapon? You should speak to your bosses
        about that. Why were they organising all the
        people to call me a coward instead of giving me
        a weapon?

A.   I don't know.

C.   You see? And everyone knew I hadn't any
        weapons, even the police. They were stopping
        all the Algerian men and searching them for
        weapons. They had them all in a group at the
        street corner with their hands up and their faces
        to the wall but they didn't stop me and why not?
        Because they had been told in advance that I

had no weapons. Because they thought I was a
European, because they wrongly thought I had
white skin because I am naturally pale because
of my studies, because I happen to have light
skin. It's not something I can help, I can't take it
off, what am I meant to do about it? Do you
want me to flay myself so I've got no skin any
more is that what you want? And then you'll see
my Algerian blood. Is that what you want?

A.   No.

C.   You say no but it is what they want. As I passed
the corner all the men shrieked coward, traitor,
coward. I was surprised the police let them
speak and paid no attention. The police let me
pass because they had information that I was
on their side. But I am an engineer. My teacher
always said I would go far if I concentrated on
my work. That's what I was doing, concentrating.
Is it a crime to work? Why should a man give up
his job and go to the hills with a bunch of
murderers? Is that what you're saying I should
have done?

A.   No.

C.   Yes. Yes that's what I should have done. So
when I came to the French Staff Headquarters
there were all the guards standing outside with
their guns, so I went up to one and shouted so
everyone could hear, I am an Algerian! I am not
a Frenchman! I am not a coward! and I grabbed
his gun. I would have killed him and then they
would have seen. So they took me away and beat
me and asked me the names of the other people
in my cell of the Maquis because they knew I
was on the side of the revolution. The police
couldn't tell I didn't know anything. They didn't
think I was a European. They knew I was an
Algerian patriot. So I was glad when they
tortured me because the voices stopped then
because everyone knew who I was. Who am I?

A.   An Algerian patriot.

C.   But for some reason they didn't kill me. I woke up here. And I think someone must have told them that I was not an Algerian because otherwise they would have killed me and that was what I wanted them to do. I hear people saying I am a coward and that I am here because I am a coward but I have been tortured and I have taken a soldier's gun. Is it you who goes about telling everyone that I'm a coward?

A.   ·   Of course not, no.

C.   You do it because you were in the Maquis so you think you're better than me.

A.   I don't at all.

C.   What did you do to be so proud about? Did you take a soldier's gun? What did you do? Why don't you answer me? Because you didn't do anything at all.

A.   I don't want to talk about it.

C.   You think I can't be trusted, is that what it is?

A.   No, it's not that.

C.   You think I'd go to the police and tell them everything because you think I'm a European pretending to be an Algerian. But I'm not. I was a little boy in the streets of the native quarter like the ones who look at me now and shout traitor at me as I go by. That was me. That is me. My teacher, Monsieur Dupont with a little beard, a very charming and interesting man, said, 'He's so clever that boy, no one would take him for a native. Work hard,' he said, 'and there are no limits to what you might become.' I have no interest in politics, do I make myself clear? So why do you think I would tell the police what you did?

A.   Please, could you stop talking to me now? I want to be quiet.

C.   Why don't you want me to talk to you? Do you think I'm a traitor? Do you think I'm not good enough to talk to you, is that it?

The NURSE *helps* B *to get out of bed. He walks slowly, supported by the* NURSE, *his look vacant.*

A.   He's walking better.

NURSE.   Yes his feet have healed up very well.

C.   I have scars to show too. I have suffered for my country too. You wouldn't think I was a European, would you, Nurse?

NURSE.   No, I'd think you were an Algerian patriot.

C.   None of you will admit it but someone in this hospital is spreading lies about me and about what I have done.

A.   I said good morning to him as usual and he turned his head to me and seemed about to speak. There was definitely a look in his eyes of noticing I was there and not being afraid.

NURSE.   We'll have him out in the garden in no time.

C.   Why won't you tell me what you did? Why won't you tell me how they hurt your hands?

A.   I have told you.

C.   No you haven't.

A.   I told you I was trying to kill myself. Don't you remember?

C.   No.

A.   You don't remember?

C.   Why don't you trust me?

A.   It's the only thing I told my wife. She didn't ask. It's safer for her not to know because there's nothing they can try to get out of her. Not that it stops them raping the women and beating them just for revenge, just for being the wife of that husband, even without knowing anything.

C.   I've been beaten.

A.   What I would say to her is, All that time when
            you never asked me where I'd been I wished
            you would. We'd eat together without saying
            anything because there was nothing we wanted
            to say except the things we couldn't. I hated you
            sometimes for being so strong and not asking
            me so I could shout, No of course I can't tell
            you. One of the things I said nothing about was
            a bar. It didn't seem very important at the time
            because there was always so much to do because
            I was working full time as a draughtsman and
            my work never suffered, I was proud of that.
            However tired I was, my work was good, and I
            even liked being praised for it by the boss
            though at the same time I would have carried
            out an order to kill him without a second
            thought, not that I disliked him particularly. So
            I carried out an order to put a bomb in a certain
            bar, which wasn't an easy job but I was
            successful and to be honest I knew I would be
            because I've always done well whatever I've tried
            to do. I'm neat to a fault, as you know, and very
            accurate. It was so successful that eight people
            were killed and about twenty wounded. I
            thought no more about it and went on with what
            came next, doing each thing as well as I could.
            There was no trouble till six months later. I was
            passing a bar – I understand what has happened
            but I suffer from it just the same. I can't talk
            about it without shaking but it's nothing I don't
            know already. I accept what has happened. I do
            try to accept that I am just going to have to put
            up with it. The second bar was just a bar, I
            passed bars all the time without thinking of the
            other one. A young Frenchman came out and
            bumped into me. Perhaps he'd had too much to
            drink or perhaps I wasn't looking where I was
            going. I had plenty on my mind even then. We
            bumped into each other and he laughed – it
            doesn't sound much, he laughed and said he was
            sorry. I couldn't say anything, I felt dizzy, and if
            I hadn't clung to him I would have fallen over.
            That night was one of the nights I couldn't sleep

and you lay awake not asking me anything. I knew it wasn't at all likely I'd killed someone like that because the bar where I left the bomb was a well-known meeting place for the most reactionary – and in any case there's always a risk that innocent people will be killed and I do accept that now. But at the time I just tried to stop thinking about it. And I succeeded. Then I was told to leave my job and go into the hills. Did you know that was what I meant when I said I was going out and didn't know when I'd be back? How long did it take you to realise I'd gone? I threw myself into my new life. It hardly seemed I was the same person who used to be a draughtsman and have a wife. I was proud of adapting so well. If there was anything extra to be done I volunteered to do it. I couldn't sleep well anyway so I deliberately went without sleep. My hands began to shake. Sometimes I felt so dizzy I could hardly do what had to be done. One day I was just sitting on the ground when every detail about the bar came into my mind so that I could see the coloured bottles and read the labels and see the face of the barman, a weak, unpleasant face. I tried to overcome the dizziness long enough to kill myself but I wasn't so successful as usual and I fainted too soon. In here it's not so easy to kill yourself. And you wouldn't want me to because after independence we may even live together again. I must just accept that I don't sleep very well and sometimes I feel that I'm dying. I do accept it. After all I would plant another bomb just the same.

C.   Have you quite finished boasting now? Why do you think I want to hear all that? Are you saying you did something I wouldn't do because you've been told I'm a coward? Are you making fun of me?

A.   Of course not.

C.   Everyone calls me a traitor and I think I'll be one in the end just to get my own back on them.

I could tell the police about you, couldn't I?
That's what they say I'm going to do.

A.   What do you mean?

C.   Can't you hear them? There are special wires
connected to this room so they can speak to me
at all times and tell me I have betrayed them.
They have told the doctors and nurses. The
doctor says when he comes in, What's wrong
with this man is he's a coward and a traitor. He
is clearly becoming a European. That's why I'm
here. Why are you here? Have you hurt your
hand? I'm here because I'm an Algerian patriot
and I was tortured but I never said a word.
Have they hurt you too? Did they hurt your
hands?

4

FANON *and the* POLICE INSPECTOR.

INSP.   My wife made me come and see you. I'm a bit
worried myself. I've always been very healthy.
You have to be strong to do a job like mine and
I can't afford to get run down. I've two little
girls to look after and everything costs money.
So I finally agreed to come and see you though
I never go to a doctor in the usual way. But it
stands to reason I'm feeling weak if I can't get
through my dinner. And if I go to bed early to
sleep it off I have nightmares, which has never
been my trouble. I never had any dreams before
and I used to think my wife was making it up
when she told me these long stories in the
morning. But I wake up in the night soaked
with sweat so I have to change my pyjamas. So I
can't keep my strength up can I, and strength is
what you need for this job. It's partly
intelligence but it's also strength. I rose to be an

inspector quite young because of those two qualities, intelligence and strength. I've always been a policeman and I wouldn't be anything else. But we're having to work too hard now. If you're conscientious, and I am, you can't go off duty when it's your turn to go off, you have to stay and see a thing through. If you don't, someone else might get the credit. It's competition like anything else. So I think tiredness is the problem. That could account for it, couldn't it? So perhaps if you just gave me a sedative.

FANON.   Account for what?

INSP.   I'm not a bad-tempered man in the normal way. What I like to do when I come home from work is sit down and have a cool drink and listen to some music on the radio and play with my little girls, and they're not bad children, I've never had to punish them. And I get on very well with my wife, I can hardly remember a quarrel since we were married and that's eight years ago. But whether it's tiredness or what it is, I get these attacks when I want to hurt people. Anyone at all who gets across me. I'm going to get on a bus and someone pushes against me in the crowd, it's probably not even his fault, I know that, and I grab him by the shoulder, my head's bursting, it's all I can do not to smash his face in. Perhaps I'm wrong to worry about it. I didn't smash his face in after all. So long as I can control myself it's nobody's business if I feel a little irritable sometimes. You'll wonder why I've come. But the trouble is it seems to be worse at home. I'm used to relaxing when I get home, letting myself go and then I can't control – To smack a child is a normal thing. It does something wrong, you say stop, she does it again, a little smack, a little cry, a little kiss, it's all over. But now, you see, if I smack one of my daughters I can't stop. I look at her little face screwed up and her fair hair I usually like so much and really I think I want to destroy her completely. I hear her cry and I'm

glad I'm making her suffer. I don't want to stop
until she's dead. And Jacqueline, that's the
younger one who is only three, was unconscious
last week for ten minutes. My wife was
screaming and hitting me to make me stop so
after I'd finished with the child I turned to her
and tied her to a chair with the cord of her
dressing gown, because this was in the morning,
you see, at breakfast-time it all happened. I said,
I'll show you the sort of man I am, and all the
time I was hitting her, you see, in the face. Then
I lit a cigarette, because we do a certain amount
with cigarettes. But Jacqueline had started to cry
again and the whole time Monique had been
howling under the table and there was so much
noise that a neighbour started banging on the
wall. That brought me back. I thought, they'll be
at the door next, so I drank my coffee which
was cold by then and went out to work without a
word. When I got back the children were
playing, my wife was cooking the dinner,
everything was the way I liked it. We had a
drink and listened to some music. Because my
life would be quite perfect if there wasn't
something the matter with me. The work's too
hard and it's getting me down. What really kills
me is the torture. No one thinks what hard work
it is for the one that's doing it. The prisoners
should have more consideration than to force us
to go on doing that to them and just tell us
quietly what we want to know. Because it's no
joke torturing someone for ten hours. You get
really involved in what you're doing. And as
often as not you get nothing out of him despite
all the work you put into it. Either they don't
know anything, but there's no way of finding
that out except by going on. Or they tell you
something that isn't true. Or if you're not good
enough at your job you may finish them off
before they've said anything at all. That's why I
do the job myself because strength is one thing
but you need intelligence too, and some of the
fellows use the Senegalese to do the work and

just sit outside having a smoke and look in every
hour to see if he's softened up yet. But the
danger is you miss the moment. Either they'll be
too gentle and get nothing out of him or more
likely they'll be too rough and kill him before
he's told you what you want. You have to keep
him just going nicely. There's a different way a
man screams at the different stages and you get
good at telling how he's going. And you can't
give up when it's going well or someone else will
be on duty when he talks and get all the credit,
so I keep on, all night if necessary and I do get
results. Though just lately my judgement's not
so good and this is all part of the trouble and I
suppose due to the lack of sleep. I get confused
when I'm tired. I mean the bodies of my wife
and children are an entirely different thing
from the jobs I have to do and I don't want to
think of the one when I'm in the other situation.
So I hope you'll be able to give me something to
calm me down so I can get on top of my work
again and enjoy my home life.

5

FANON *and the* YOUNG DOCTOR.

DOCTOR.   I was right, you see. She had penicillin in her
bag. The police were called at once and whisked
her away so we're short of a nurse but not so
short of supplies. It's better to keep out of
politics. I'm not sure I'd even like to get
involved helping the police though it's a very
good thing to have a doctor standing by to look
after the patient between sessions because
otherwise they might kill him. If you keep giving
him injections of vitamins it does help keep him
alive which can only be a good thing. As a
matter of fact I have been approached by the

police superintendent for help with psychiatric methods such as injections of Pentothal as a truth drug and I do think that would be interesting work. It's an opportunity to learn more about how successful these drugs are in liberating the patient from the conflict that prevents him speaking, because a prisoner of course is very highly motivated not to speak. And it's most important to see whether this can be done without too great subsequent damage to the personality. We'll probably have them here as patients afterwards so we can observe the effects. But even allowing for side effects there'll be far less suffering overall than if electricity were used and the most important thing for a doctor is to save the patient from suffering. I think one can go to the prisoner in all honesty and say, I am a doctor, I am not a policeman, I am here to help you. And then when he's relaxed and has confidence in you, you can give him an intravenous injection of Pentothal, the interrogation takes places smoothly and easily, and a great deal of suffering is avoided. So I think I needn't hesitate in accepting that offer. I think one must do everything one can to lessen the suffering of this war and bring it to an end as quickly as possible. Because without us they'd go back to the Middle Ages but they have got a future as Frenchmen if they'll only accept it. My father's barns are repeatedly set alight and yet I don't give up hope. A patient comes to see you and he can't even tell you where the pain is. You can't be a doctor with a native, if you have to be a vet. And when you've found what's wrong with him he goes off with the medicine and drinks it all in one gulp and expects to be made better instantly. And he goes to his magician for his medicine too, little cuts on the forehead and killing a hen. It's as if they don't trust a proper doctor who is doing all he can to help them. But I don't despair. It all brings out the adventurer in me, I find. My father made his farm from wild country and you can't make roads through

swamps without men dying. Stirring times.
Meanwhile one must alleviate suffering
wherever one can so I'll give my reply to the
superintendent today. Don't you agree? You
don't agree do you? It's beginning to be clear
that, for all this Parisian air, it's beginning to be
clear what your feelings are. I'm not slow to spot
these things. I've just been proved right in the
case of a certain nurse. I'm not threatening you,
a friend's a friend, but it does worry me to see
the way your mind's working. Naturally, with
your racial background you identify perhaps
with the Algerian but I promise you and I've
lived here all my life the Algerian peasant is
nothing at all like you. Well, as I always say let's
keep politics out of the hospital. I just hope very
much I never meet you as one of the
superintendent's patients.

6

FANON, MONSIEUR, MADAMEE *and* FRANÇOISE.

MADAME. Doctor, Doctor, I beg you –

    Silence.

MONSIEUR. Well here you are. I suppose we have you to
    thank.

FANON.   What for?

MONSIEUR (*indicating* FRANÇOISE). This. This.

FANON.   Good morning, Françoise.

    MADAME *laughs shrilly.*

    Françoise.

MONSIEUR. Three days she hasn't spoken.

MADAME. Spoken? Spoken? Moved! She hasn't moved a

finger for three days. She might be dead except that she's breathing.

MONSIEUR. She could move if she wanted to. I think it's deliberate. I sometimes think so. I tell you, Doctor, I don't know what to think.

MADAME. She's resisting us, that's what it is. You're perfectly right to say it's deliberate. It's sheer wilful obstinacy, it can't be anything else, except that clearly she is mad, she is completely, completely mad, she should be here in hospital.

MONSIEUR. I insist that she's admitted this morning. It's more than anyone should be asked to bear. Do you understand that? If you can't understand me I insist on speaking to your superiors. Who is in charge of this hospital? I am not an ordinary person to be pushed about in this way. I am a member of the administration. I have seen native patients in the garden and am I to understand that they have been admitted and you are refusing to admit my daughter?

FANON. Please sit down. Please calm yourself. Could you tell me how your daughter has been since I saw her last? Has she been eating?

MADAME. Only when she thinks we're not watching. If I go out of the room and leave her with a plate of food under her nose, after a while she will eat something. I can tell you see by some of the food having gone. Or sometimes I watch through a crack in the door. I've stood there for hours without making a sound, watching her, and she sits in her chair just staring and not moving a muscle. It's not natural. It's more than anyone should be asked to bear. It's all right for my husband, he goes out all day, and I'm alone in the house with this terrifying silent person in the chair. Hour after hour.

MONSIEUR. All right for me? Do you know how my work has suffered? I can't remember names and faces, I can't concentrate on what I'm doing, all the time I'm thinking about that child and I don't spare myself, I travel about the region, I talk, I question, I – work very hard and when I get home I am exhausted and what do I find? No dinner, my wife in hysterics, the girl has to be carried up to bed like a baby.

MADAME.   No dinner? When was there no dinner?

MONSIEUR. When? When has dinner been ready?

MADAME.   What time do you come in? How do I know when to have it ready?

MONSIEUR. Is this the sort of support I get from you? It's for you and Françoise I'm working till all hours saving this country from itself.

MADAME.   For me? I don't want it. They can keep it. I'd go back to France tomorrow. I would, I would. I hate it here. I've always hated it.

MONSIEUR. Think what you're saying.

MADAME.   I do, I hate it. It's too hot and it's smelly and there are flies and all these filthy natives, no better than animals, worse because I like animals –

MONSIEUR. It's my country, it's mine.

MADAME.   Yes you like it, you like a bit of filth. You say you're bringing them French culture, all those volumes of Proust in the bookcase and Racine and Corneille, you and Françoise were always great ones for quoting poetry, that's very fine, but really you like what's exotic, what you would call exotic, you like a bit of highly spiced food and smells of the bazaar and the women in their yashmaks, and you'd like nothing better than to get your hands under a yashmak and I bet you've done it in your time, you filthy Algerian pig. I'd go back to France tomorrow.

FANON.   I know this is all very distressing for you.

MONSIEUR. Go then. Go back to France. Go on. Go back now. I'm staying here. This is my country. They'll have to kill me before they drive me out. I take my stand. I am already in France. Algeria is France.

MADAME. Of course in a manner of speaking it is France.

MONSIEUR. In every sense of the word it is France. So you see. I must ask you, Doctor, to forgive us. I think I can safely say we have never had a quarrel in eighteen years of marriage. We live under great strain.

MADAME. This terrible war.

MONSIEUR. The strain of Françoise's illness.

MADAME. Yes, that is a terrible strain.

FANON. You say she has been like this for three days. Before that, how was she?

MADAME. Worse. (*She laughs.*) Oh yes, it's better to have her like this really.

FANON. In what way worse?

MONSIEUR. Raving. Raving mad.

MADAME. She kept getting out of the house and going and telling our neighbours we were doing all kinds of terrible things, killing people and so forth, really. (*She laughs.*) I know it sounds incredible but she did, and that we were keeping her prisoner of all things. Even when we locked her up she escaped and set off again talking to anyone she met and asking for help but luckily she was so clearly mad that no one believed a word she said. I mean, for instance, she would say that she was dead (*She laughs.*) so obviously.

MONSIEUR. Terrible terrible times.

MADAME. There was one occasion – I may tell the doctor, mayn't I, dear? Shall I tell the doctor what she did?

MONSIEUR. Do what you like. Do what's necessary.

MADAME. It was her birthday you see and I'd made her a lovely dress and we'd had lots of fittings and really in a way it was like old times because she didn't say anything nasty while we were doing the dress. It was blue, not dark blue and not

pale blue either, a nice clear blue that she's
always liked since she was a little girl and it's a
colour that seems absolutely Françoise to me.
She was being so good really we thought we
might have some very old friends to see us, who
knew about our trouble and were terribly
concerned for us. Françoise hadn't got out for
two days and things weren't going too badly
except for the wicked things she would suddenly
shout out about her daddy when she didn't
know what she was saying, and she wasn't quite
all she should be about using the toilet I'm
ashamed to say but we won't say anything about
that. So I got Françoise all dressed and did her
hair prettily, I'd washed it the night before, and
tied it back with a piece of ribbon the very shade
of the dress, I had quite a search to find it but
important things are worth a bit of effort, and
then I went downstairs to greet our friends. My
husband was home early, we all sat down, it was
so delightful for a short time. I called Françoise.
And when she came downstairs what do you
think? You won't believe what she'd done. She
had taken her dress off. And not just her dress I
may say. Not even my husband has ever seen me
in the state Françoise walked into that room and
sat down in a chair. In broad daylight. In the
living-room. In front of us and in front of our
old friends. Nobody could help seeing her. Of
course we all screamed. She paid not the
slightest attention. I shouted to her to go out of
the room and get dressed but she pretended not
to hear a word I said. I grabbed her arm but she
was quite rigid. So at last I snatched up some
cushions and covered her with those. Then my
husband took our guests out of the room and I
went to get some clothes to dress her in. But her
beautiful blue dress was cut to pieces and she
had gone to the toilet all over it. So she had to
wear an ordinary dress. And from that moment
on she hasn't said a word. However much I
shout and cry and beg her to talk she won't say
anything at all. But really I think it's better that

she doesn't if all she can say is what she was
saying before. I just hope you know what to do
with her.

MONSIEUR. But I believe in French culture. I believe in
Racine and Proust. A day will come – A few of
them can understand it. You yourself, Doctor,
have risen above your race. But for the most
part they must be beaten because they resist us
and go on and on resisting us however hard we
force – and what about us? Our lives? Aren't we
to live? I was born here, do you see? What will
become of me if I have to go? What will I be? I
don't want to go. (*He cries.*)

MADAME. Take no notice.

MONSIEUR. I don't want to go. I won't go. I will stay here.
And Françoise was a clever child and she would
have grown up to be – (*He cries some more.*)

MADAME. Take no notice. It's much the best thing.

MONSIEUR. Doctor, help me because I'm finished. I've tried
so hard and nobody helps me. What about me?
(*He cries.*)

MADAME. He wouldn't want you to take any notice. He'll
be himself in a moment.

MONSIEUR. What about me?

MADAME. He'll be himself in a moment. We must just take
no notice. We must go home and Françoise must
be taken care of here. You'll be keeping her
here I gather, Doctor?

FANON. Yes your daughter had better be admitted to
hospital. Schizophrenia is a very common form
of madness about which not a great deal is
known. I'm afraid I can't say at this stage what
the prospects are of her recovery.

MADAME. I'm sure Françoise will get better at once as soon
as she has proper treatment in hospital. After all
being mad is an illness these days and with
wonderful modern drugs – I think modern

medicine is so wonderful and science and indeed
all of western civilisation and I think we are so
lucky to live when and where we do and not in
some dark age or place. I do believe firmly in
progress and Françoise will be her old self again.

MONSIEUR. We'll look forward very much to welcoming
her home again when she's better. And let's
hope that is in a pacified French Algeria, the
country I want my child to inherit.

MADAME. That's so beautifully put that it's sure to happen.
I feel full of confidence, Doctor, now that
everything is in your hands.

MONSIEUR. Well now I have a lot of work to do. A great
deal of time has been wasted the last few weeks
with all the distractions but now I can forge
ahead. Thank you Doctor and goodbye.

MADAME. We are grateful to you, Doctor, from the bottom
of our hearts and I'm sure Françoise is too if she
were only able to say so. Perhaps in just a few
weeks all this horrid trouble will be over.
Mummy will come in visiting hours, Francie. Do
you think she hears me? Is she conscious in our
sense of the word? I quite wish I was a doctor
and could see into her head. Take care of my
baby won't you?

They go.

FANON. Françoise.

He takes her gently by the arm and leads her out.

7

The ward: three beds. The middle bed, B's, is empty. C is in bed, A is standing.

C. You're going home?

A.	Yes, tomorrow morning.
C.	If I had a wife I would be going home but I don't think my parents want to see me because of certain misunderstandings so that they don't altogether realise what a large part I have played in the revolution.
A.	That's a pity.
C.	I've been writing letters to them but in the present state of things they're not delivered because someone has told the post office that I'm a traitor and my letters are stopped.
A.	My wife hasn't visited me the last three days.
C.	I suppose they can tell by my handwriting, though it doesn't look to me like the handwriting of a traitor.
A.	Yes I shall go home for a few days and then wherever I'm told to go.

FANON *comes in*.

FANON	(*to* A). You were planning to leave tomorrow morning?
A.	Is there any reason why not?
C.	Why do you keep me here, Doctor? You keep me here as if I was in prison. The things you've been told about me are all lies and I can prove to you that I'm an Algerian –
FANON.	Yes. Yes I know. You will go home soon. You need more rest. (*To* A.) Excuse me, I must talk to you privately. (*He takes* A *aside*.)
A.	What's the matter?
FANON.	After your discharge from hospital you are going to join the Maquis again?
A.	Yes. I know what I'm doing.
FANON.	Were you going home first?
A.	I want a few days with my wife and then I'll go wherever they send me till it's all over.

FANON. I have some bad news. I'm sorry. I've just been given a message that your wife is dead.

A. Because of me?

FANON. No, no. No. Not that at all. She was carrying explosives and she tripped and fell.

A. Was she? Yes.

FANON. It might be better if you stayed here a few more days.

A. There's no need. That's very kind. There's no need.

FANON. I think it would be better.

A. No I must go straight away to join my friends. I must go now at once.

FANON. You are not due to be discharged till tomorrow.

A. Of course, yes. Tomorrow. I wonder how long she's been doing that.

FANON. You had no idea?

A. No, she'd learnt not to talk to me. I didn't talk to her. It was simpler like that because there would have been so much to say. I thought I would tell her after independence. You don't happen to know if she died at once?

FANON. The message didn't say.

A. But it seems likely, doesn't it?

FANON. Almost certain.

C. What are you saying about me?

FANON. Nothing about you.

C. I heard my name mentioned in the context of the revolution.

FANON. And where is our other friend?

A. In the garden. He goes in the garden now.

FANON. Of course he does.

C.   Why are you black, Doctor?

FANON.   Why?

C.   It's done to insult me. You are deliberately black
            to make me look white. You want to make me
            look like a Frenchman. I will not look like a
            Frenchman for you or anyone else, is that clear?
            What am I meant to do with my skin? It is not
            my skin in any case but all due to a
            misunderstanding which I hope is going to be
            cleared up by the authorities. Because it is
            perfectly clear in spite of your alleged blackness
            that I am an Algerian patriot and I have
            suffered for my country and I will not have you
            spreading lies about me to the other patients.

FANON.   I do not spread lies about you.

C.   You mean you think it's true what they say? You
            must not believe a word of it. I am the only one
            who can tell you the actual truth of the situation.
            I would tell you what I am if I were sure you
            could be trusted. Another time perhaps if you
            apply through the proper channels.

8

The POLICE INSPECTOR *is lying down on a trolley-bed, very
white, eyes closed, face covered with sweat.*
FANON *gives him an injection.*
After a moment, the POLICE INSPECTOR *opens his eyes.*

INSP.   Has he gone?

FANON.   Who?

INSP.   It's not fair when I'd pulled myself together.
            You don't want to see them afterwards. He
            never talked either, the bastard. I don't think he
            knew anything. What's he doing here?

FANON.   Who?

INSP.   I saw him just now in the hospital garden. I got here a bit early for my appointment so I thought I'd take a turn round the garden. Then I saw him coming between the trees. I woke up in here. Was he really there? I haven't started seeing things that aren't there? Doctor?

FANON.   Who was it?

INSP.   I was in charge of his interrogation. A small man about fifty. A mole on his cheek. I wouldn't forget a man I'd tortured. I paid attention to him at the time and I know things about him his mother wouldn't know. He's a patient here? Is he?

FANON.   Yes, he is.

INSP.   What's the matter with him? Is he mad? He always seemed a bit strange to me. You get them and you think they're terrorists and they're just some harmless lunatic, that has happened.

FANON.   He's not mad. He was perfectly well when you first met him. He's suffering from shock.

INSP.   Well I'm the one who had the shock, I can tell you. I still feel all weak in the legs. I'm not getting better as fast as I should, Doctor. I still get angry and I can't stop myself – should I send my wife and children away?

FANON.   If your superiors refuse to give you sick leave I see only one possible way for you to get better.

INSP.   I don't altogether blame them. They're very short of men and I'm still better than a lot of people at the specialist work we do. Even though I'm not at my best. You have to have a flair for it and I have got a flair.

FANON.   But you know don't you that the symptoms you complain of are caused by these interrogations you do so well?

INSP.   It's a strain, I admit. But the troubles altogether

at the moment. I don't know that you can single
out one thing more than another at a time like
this.

FANON.   I think in your case we can single out your work
and if you're asking me to cure you I
recommend you to ask to be transferred to some
other branch of police work.

INSP.   That's nonsense. There's no way of evading that
kind of duty. You're as good as saying I'd have
to leave the force altogether.

FANON.   Yes, I would recommend that.

INSP.   You can't say that. It's not a possibility at all.
You'll have to find some other solution. What
am I then if I'm not a policeman? I've always
been a policeman. You're asking something out
of the question.

FANON.   I'm sorry but it's all I can suggest.

INSP.   Come on now. You're the doctor. What about all
these medicines? You gave me something just
now that made me feel a whole lot better very
quickly.

FANON.   I can give you sedatives to help you sleep. I can
give you tranquillisers to take during the day.

INSP.   You've been doing that already and I don't
mean I'm not grateful but it's just not good
enough. I want to be back in tip top condition
and lead a normal life.

FANON.   I'll renew your prescription.

INSP.   It's no joke having nightmares like I do. It's easy
enough for you, Doctor, sitting here doing your
job. Your job doesn't make you ill.

FANON.'   I'll see you in a fortnight.

9

A, C *and the* MALE NURSE.
A *and* C *are in bed.* B's *bed is empty.*
A *is staring into space.*
FANON *comes in.*

FANON.   Nurse, where is this patient?

NURSE.   In the garden. Yes, he usually comes back at
            about this time.

FANON.   I'd like to make sure he's all right because I've
            just been talking to another patient who –

            They go out together.

C.   When it is fully understood that I am not a
            traitor or a coward but an Algerian patriot then
            I can go back to my work again because the
            machinery is waiting for my attention. It will not
            be French machinery, that is perfectly clear, but
            I will not be asked to think about politics
            because I am an engineer and it is no good you
            constantly saying to me that I am a coward and
            a traitor because I will build such bridges and I
            will design such revolutionary machinery for all
            the factories of a free country so it would not be
            in anyone's interests if I were to go and get
            killed now by joining in any fighting because I
            have already proved to everyone's satisfaction
            that I am the man who took a gun from a
            French soldier and I am not a –

            FANON *and the* NURSE *come in, bringing* B.

B.   No no no no no.

NURSE.   Come along, it's all right, come along.

FANON.   I don't think he's done himself any harm. His
            neck isn't marked. He was certainly trying to
            hang himself but he's far too shocked to manage
            it.

C.   Why does he get all the attention? Who's the
            Algerian patriot?

B.   No no no. Don't let him take me back. Let me
            die. I can't go back there.

FANON.   The man you saw is a patient here. He hasn't
            come to take you away. He's a patient who
            comes to see me. Do you understand? The
            police don't come into the hospital. The police
            will not come here. The man you saw was not a
            policeman coming to arrest you. He was a patient
            coming to see me. He has gone now. He has gone
            home. All right? Do you understand? You are
            here to be looked after. No one's going to take
            you away. You're safe in bed in hospital. There.
            No one's going to hurt you. You need plenty of
            rest. You rest there in bed. You're safe there.

            When B is quiet, FANON goes out.
            The NURSE stays by B.
            Silence.

C.   Haven't I suffered for my country?

10

FRANÇOISE *and* FANON.

At first they sit in silence.

FRANÇOISE. The dress looked very pretty but underneath I
            was rotting away. Bit by bit I was disappearing.
            The dress is walking about with no one inside it. I
            undo the buttons and put my hand in. Under the
            dress I can't find where I am. So when I take it
            off there's nobody there. They can't see
            Françoise because she was taken off upstairs and
            nobody came downstairs and into the room. My
            mother made that dress to kill me. It ate me
            away. That was a poison dress I put on.

THE JUDGE'S WIFE

Characters

JUDGE, 60s
CAROLINE, his wife, about 60
BARBARA, Caroline's sister, 60s
PEG, the Judge's maid, 20s
VERNON WARREN, a young man
MICHAEL WARREN, his brother
WARREN'S MOTHER, 50s

The Judge's Wife was first transmitted on BBC 2, on 2 October 1972 with the following cast:

JUDGE	Sebastian Shaw
CAROLINE	Rachel Kempson
BARBARA	Valerie White
PEG	Evin Crowley
MICHAEL WARREN } VERNON WARREN }	Anthony Andrews
WARREN'S MOTHER	Grace Dolan

Directed by James Fearman

An old man, the JUDGE, *is lying shot dead in a wood.*
The JUDGE *and a young man,* MICHAEL WARREN, *are*
standing in the wood. WARREN *shoots the* JUDGE. *The* JUDGE
is lying dead exactly as before. A car stops at the edge of the wood.
The JUDGE *and* WARREN *get out and walk into the wood. Then*
an exact repeat of them standing in the wood, WARREN *shooting*
the JUDGE, *the* JUDGE *lying dead.*
A close-up of the JUDGE, *alive, in his wig.*

JUDGE.   Every criminal is a revolutionary. And every
           revolutionary is a criminal. For they both act in
           defiance of laws that protect us, protect our
           property, protect what we in this society have
           chosen to be. And whether a man who comes
           against the forces of law and order presents
           himself to us as a criminal or as a revolutionary
           is irrelevant. In either case he is challenging our
           society. And he must take the heavy
           consequences. For our society is upheld by force
           and we should not be afraid to admit it. The
           forces of law and order are stronger than those
           of revolt and we will not hesitate to use our
           strength.

           We have police to do what we want done. They
           are armed with truncheons, dogs, horses, cars,
           gas sometimes and sometimes guns. If necessary
           we have the army, and there is no limit to the
           force that could in theory be brought to bear
           against the country's enemies. To eliminate the
           entire population would be impractical but not
           impossible and goes to show that it is not
           strength we lack. So why do we pretend? Why
           do we not say plainly that we will use any means
           necessary to keep things the way they are? We
           will never be intimidated. Your violence will be
           met by violence and we are stronger than you.

           A close-up of VERNON WARREN, *the accused.*
           His face is calm and doesn't change while the JUDGE
           speaks.

           Vernon Warren, you have attempted to
           overthrow the established institutions of this
           realm and you have urged others to do so. That

you have failed in this shameful enterprise is due to your own ineptitude and the great vigilance of the police. But are you to be rewarded for this failure with a light sentence so that you may rest for a while at the state's expense perfecting your schemes and try to do better a second time?

A close-up of the JUDGE.

No, you must be punished according to your intention.

WARREN's MOTHER *is standing in her kitchen. She is in her fifties, shapeless, lined, tired. Tears are running down her face.*

A close-up of PEG, *an Irish girl in her twenties, her hair tied back off her face, wearing an apron.*

PEG.   That was a heavy sentence, sir.

PEG, *the* JUDGE *and* CAROLINE, *the* JUDGE's *wife, are in the hall of the house. The* JUDGE *has just come in.* CAROLINE *has come to meet him.* PEG *stands further off, by the door to the kitchen.*

CAROLINE. Go, go back to the kitchen at once. How dare you speak to the Judge like that?

JUDGE.   We shall have no more Irish girls.

The JUDGE *is standing in the bathroom by the bath, which is running.* CAROLINE *undresses him. He is completely passive. He stands naked, fat, old, defenceless.*

WARREN *is sitting at a kitchen table with uneaten food. After a moment he looks round, half draws a gun out of his pocket, slips it back. His* MOTHER *comes in. She has been crying. She puts her arm round* WARREN *and he leans his head against her.*

PEG *is banging veal escalopes in the kitchen, and goes on banging while* CAROLINE *talks.*

CAROLINE. You're very lucky he managed to keep his temper. I hope you realise that. The judge is

exhausted. He has been listening for twelve
days. I'm sure you never listen for five minutes.
His summing up took fourteen hours. Could
you speak intelligently for fourteen hours? At a
time like this he needs our support and comfort.
Try to make up for your insolence by cooking a
perfect dinner and all may yet be forgiven.

PEG goes on banging.

The JUDGE *is lying in the bath, his eyes closed. The
phone rings, off. He opens his eyes.*

CAROLINE *(lifting the phone).* Yes? (*She listens a moment,
closing her eyes, then puts the receiver down.*)

The JUDGE *is wide-eyed in the bath.* CAROLINE
*comes in, holds out a large towel for him. He gets out.
She wraps him in it. They start out of the bathroom.
He slips on the wet floor and almost falls.*

JUDGE.   Damn your eyes, Caroline, be more careful.

The JUDGE *and* CAROLINE's *bedroom: twin beds,
a dressing-table, a small portable TV on the table. We
can see the screen but only as one of many things in
the room, not close up. The sound is low but audible.
The* JUDGE's *clothes are laid out on the bed.*

TV.   At the Old Bailey today Vernon Warren, leader
of the –

The JUDGE *turns the sound right down. The TV
shows stills of* VERNON WARREN *and the*
JUDGE, *film of demonstrators with placards, arrests,
scuffles, general violence. This is never close up, but
in a small intense corner of the large, still bedroom
where the* JUDGE *goes on slowly getting dressed, not
looking at the TV.* CAROLINE *helps but he is more
active now and sometimes pushes her off irritably,
tying his own tie. When he is dressed he goes out of the
room. When he has gone* CAROLINE *looks at the
TV but it is on to a different item.*

BARBARA *meets the* JUDGE *on the stairs. He
starts, then indifferent, cold, nods impatiently. She
stops and looks at him hard with dislike, watches him*

go down, then goes on up.

BARBARA and CAROLINE are in the bedroom.
BARBARA's face is in profile. We see CAROLINE
full-face in the mirror of the dressing-table, and the
back of her head. She is sitting at the dressing-table
making up her face. They are sisters and both about
sixty. They have similar faces but BARBARA, with
no make-up, short untidy hair, and indifferent clothes,
is an old woman. CAROLINE, as she makes up,
looks far younger, bland, without character.

BARBARA. Do you always agree with what he does?

CAROLINE. Oh yes.

BARBARA. I know Warren had to be found guilty. But
weren't you at all shocked by the sentence?

CAROLINE. Shocked? by the sentence? I was shocked by the
crimes.

BARBARA. Yes, Laurence said he was shocked by the
crimes.

CAROLINE. I am his wife, Barbara. You don't seem to
understand about marriage.

BARBARA. If you thought he was wrong would you say so?
Or does his wife keep quiet?

CAROLINE. Sentencing is his job. It's a very technical
matter. I wouldn't expect to know if he did it
wrong. Some other expert might. My job is
looking after him.

BARBARA. Are you frightened of him?

CAROLINE. What a funny idea, Barbara. Are you?

BARBARA. What would he do to you if you said what you
really think?

CAROLINE. But I really think he's absolutely right. Don't
start on politics, please darling, or he won't sleep
tonight and nor will I.

BARBARA turns away.
CAROLINE looks at herself steadily and miserably.

She smiles radiantly, holds it for a moment, then lets it go and stares at herself as before.

The living-room.

The JUDGE *is striking matches and putting them out between his finger and thumb. The phone rings. He answers with a grunt. After a moment he hangs up. He sits impassive.*

CAROLINE, *holding a small dog, is watching the* JUDGE. BARBARA *is also watching him. He starts striking matches again.*

CAROLINE. I don't see why we don't get the police to tap the phone and find out where he is and deal with him in the proper way.

WARREN *comes out of phone-box, gets into cab (the same one as at the beginning) and drives off.*

Back in the living-room.

CAROLINE. I've always said our number should be ex-directory. We get these endless calls from cranks of all sorts.

JUDGE. I like to hear how I'm hated. I wouldn't be doing my job if everyone liked me.

BARBARA. You've gone too far this time, Laurence. I used to think you were an old fool but meant well. Now I think you're bloody dangerous.

JUDGE (*to* CAROLINE). Tell your sister that a plain old spinster doesn't make herself more interesting by being rude. And give me another whisky larger than the last one. And tell that slut in the kitchen that last night's dinner was so incompetent that I suspect her of deliberate sabotage.

BARBARA. If you want to hear how you're hated you should get her to tell you some time.

CAROLINE. Barbara, you haven't been talking to the cook?

BARBARA. The number of sharp knives she has in there I'm surprised you can sleep.

CAROLINE (*giving the* JUDGE *whisky*). Barbara, how can you?

JUDGE. The good girl is angry with me for being so horrid to the pretty young man. There's no death sentence unfortunately. No one is being flogged. Do you think your whining, Barbara, has any effect on me? I know your namby-pamby politics. Do you think I care if five thousand people are out tonight rioting in protest at my sentence? Ha, I only wish I had made it double.

WARREN is driving the car with the JUDGE *beside him. The car pulls up by the edge of the wood.* *WARREN and the* JUDGE *get out exactly as before, the whole sequence being repeated till the* JUDGE *is lying dead.*

The JUDGE, CAROLINE, *and* BARBARA *are sitting at the dinner-table. There is soup in their bowls but only* CAROLINE *has started to eat.*

JUDGE. I shall retire to a remote island.

BARBARA. I wish you would.

JUDGE. I will. The west of Scotland. Guillemots. Cormorants. Shag.

CAROLINE. There are things one would miss. Not people perhaps.

JUDGE. There's no shortage of whisky in Scotland.

CAROLINE. I wonder if Harrods would deliver?

BARBARA. In fact, you'll dodder on till you're eighty and completely senile with all your judgements reversed by the Court of Appeal.

JUDGE. Do you know that's never happened to me yet?

BARBARA. It will now. They'll halve Warren's sentence.

JUDGE. My judgements stand.

CAROLINE. Which island have you in mind, Laurence?

BARBARA. Laurence, I don't defend violence. I am a

pacifist, as you know very well.

JUDGE. More fool you. What are people that you should mind them being killed? Look about you when you walk down the street. Such faces. Which of them would stop to save you? They would see you dead, Barbara, and me, and Caroline, and anyone except each his own little family, and most murders, of course, are precisely of husbands and wives or gassing the children. I don't know why death should be an issue. Think of the deaths on the road. If cars are worth all that slaughter almost any cause however bad must be worth a few people dead.

BARBARA. I'm only saying that I don't defend violence but I still don't think that Warren's crimes, though I agree they are crimes of violence, though I have every sympathy with the victims –

CAROLINE. Whatever you may say about Peg, she does make delicious vichyssoise.

JUDGE. Will you not interrupt me?

CAROLINE. I think we will spoil our appetite if we talk about work at dinner.

JUDGE. Spoil our appetite? Who has an appetite for this muck? Call the girl in.

CAROLINE. Ah no, it's delicious soup, isn't it Barbara?

BARBARA. Yes the soup's fine, Laurence, we can talk and drink our soup.

JUDGE. We can't drink this. It tastes of nothing but salt.

BARBARA. You put that in yourself.

CAROLINE. Let me taste.

JUDGE. Take the stuff away.

CAROLINE. Why you've put in far too much salt, you silly old thing. Have mine.

JUDGE. Call the girl in here. I shall call her. Peg is it? Peg. Peg.

CAROLINE. This is your fault, Barbara. It is. I've warned
and warned you not to criticise.

PEG comes in.

JUDGE.   What is this? What do you call it?

PEG.   Vichyssoise soup, sir.

JUDGE.   It is sea water, Peg.

CAROLINE. The judge has accidentally put in a little too
much salt.

JUDGE.   And without the salt what would it be? It would
be Irish bog water. I know you mad Irish live
off potatoes but I don't want potato and bog
water served up as soup in my house. Take it
away. Take it all away.

BARBARA. I should like to finish mine.

JUDGE.   I said take it away.

PEG clears away the soup and goes out.
The phone rings.
The JUDGE doesn't get up.
CAROLINE sits looking down at the table.
BARBARA watches the JUDGE.
The phone goes on ringing.
The JUDGE gets up suddenly, picks up the receiver
and at once puts it down again.

BARBARA. Why don't you retire? I think that's a good idea.

JUDGE.   And live alone on an island with this cow? Don't
think while you eat or you won't sleep. Don't
talk while you sleep or you won't eat. Don't
think while you talk.

CAROLINE. This case has taken it out of you.

JUDGE.   And why shouldn't it? I was trying my right to
exist, don't you know that? Warren is what is
happening to us. His speeches and pamphlets
are stirring this country up to a new idea of
what is possible. It is for me to show that it is
not possible. To put out this fire with my hands.

PEG comes in with a tray of food.

What's this?

PEG.   Escalope of veal, sir. And I hope it chokes you.

CAROLINE. Peg! No, no, Laurence, don't hurt her.

The JUDGE *hasn't moved towards* PEG. *He is just looking at her.*

Peg, run back to the kitchen.

JUDGE.   Have you ever tried to poison me?

PEG   (*still putting the food on the table*). I've thought of it many times. I'll be leaving now and I won't come back again. I won't be working for anyone at all. It was my mistake ever to come to England. I'm going home tomorrow.

CAROLINE. Go away, Peg, go back to the kitchen.

PEG   (*to the* JUDGE). Not till I tell you what I think of you. You remind me of a toad I saw one time run over by a tractor. It was sitting there like you swelled up and ugly and then there was nothing left of it at all.

The JUDGE *gets into the car with* WARREN. WARREN *is driving the car. The whole sequence is repeated exactly as before until the* JUDGE *is lying dead in the wood.*

The food is uneaten on the plates.
The JUDGE, CAROLINE *and* BARBARA *are sitting in the living-room, silently, with drinks. There are footsteps in the hall. The front door bangs shut.*

CAROLINE. I wonder what she's stolen.

BARBARA. You can't be surprised.

CAROLINE. I'm always surprised when people don't like me. I do like to be liked. How nice it would be to be liked by everyone.

JUDGE.   Our duty is to be hated if necessary.

BARBARA. But you do stir up such ill feeling. You go out of your way. I think Vernon Warren's

movement would simply die out if left to itself
and reforms would come as they do in England
slowly but surely and without any violence. But
you're making him a martyr. Every worker,
every black, every student thinks tonight he
might even die for Warren and quite a few will
feel the same tomorrow and some actually will
die for him.

JUDGE.   Do you think so?

BARBARA. Didn't you see the size of the demonstration?
And that was just what happened spontaneously,
the few people outside the court. They'll
organise something big at the weekend. You are
so stupid, Laurence.

JUDGE.   Hundreds of them will be arrested. And given
heavy sentences.

BARBARA. And then?

The phone rings.
The JUDGE *answers, listens.*

JUDGE.   I'm not afraid, you know.

He hangs up.

BARBARA. You should talk to Thomas.

CAROLINE. We don't want to talk to our children, thank
you very much. We do our best to avoid that
sort of thing.

BARBARA. He agrees with me I'm sure.

JUDGE.   I don't know what sort of socialist Thomas is.
He's as plump as any conservative I know. He
does just manage to use state schools and that's
his greatest sacrifice so far. I think socialist is
something he calls himself to annoy me. But I'm
not interested enough to be annoyed. I would
rather not have had children. I would rather not
have been born. I would rather the apes had
stayed in the trees.

WARREN *is sitting in the parked car in the dark.*

Back to the living-room, as before, but now
CAROLINE *has a tray of coffee and is pouring it
out.*

CAROLINE. Will coffee keep you awake?

JUDGE. I shall never sleep again. Give me the coffee.

CAROLINE. He keeps me awake too, I'm not allowed to
sleep if he can't sleep.

BARBARA. I seem to think when you were young,
Laurence, you weren't so hateful. Spiky, yes, but
Caroline and I liked spiky men. You couldn't get
hold of them too easily. You weren't very bright
about politics but you certainly weren't this
right-wing buffoon. Jack the Ripper of the
Queen's Bench. I lived abroad so much I lost
track. But even twenty years ago you were quite
ordinary. It's since then. Did power corrupt like
it's supposed to?

JUDGE. Go away Barbara. I've had enough. Should we
all be kind? You are lukewarm and will be
vomited. There are two camps, Barbara, mine
and theirs. Either you are with, or you are
against.

BARBARA. I do dislike that silly way of talking.

JUDGE. You know nothing. You only see yourself. You
never married. You never lived. You will die
without having been born.

BARBARA. I never married you and I would kill myself if I
was in Caroline's position now.

CAROLINE. You were never asked to marry him.

BARBARA. Yes, I was.

CAROLINE. I don't believe you and we're too old now for
jealousy.

JUDGE. I asked her and it's lucky she said no because I
don't like antiseptic mouthwash, I like a drink.

The phone rings. The JUDGE *lets it ring while he
pours himself a drink, then answers.*

JUDGE.   I should like very much to see you face to face. I
            should like to see which of us was frightened.
            (*He listens a bit more then hangs up.*)

BARBARA. None of us has done all we might have done.

JUDGE.   I have done everything possible. You haven't,
            no. Be maudlin, yes, it suits you, Barbara.

CAROLINE. When was it you asked her to marry you?

JUDGE.   (*to* BARBARA). When this country runs with
            blood I shall go down fighting. I hope to see
            you killed in the crossfire.

CAROLINE. More coffee, Barbara.

JUDGE.   Caroline, I'm going out for a walk.

CAROLINE. A walk?

JUDGE.   Yes, and without a scarf.

CAROLINE. Will you take the dog?

JUDGE.   No.

CAROLINE. He needs to go. Peg isn't here to do it.

JUDGE.   I do not want the dog. Let him piss on the
            carpet.

BARBARA. I shouldn't walk about too much, Laurence. It
            may not be safe. You aren't very popular.

JUDGE.   I am unpopular because I choose to be. If I
            wanted to be popular, how I would be loved.

            He goes out.
            BARBARA *and* CAROLINE *are sitting side by side
            on the sofa in silence.*

            Another road.
            The JUDGE *walks on.*
            As before, the JUDGE *gets into the car with*
            WARREN *and the sequence is repeated until the*
            JUDGE *lies dead in the wood.*
            A still of the JUDGE *lying dead in the wood on the
            front page of a newspaper.*
            It is the next day. CAROLINE *is sitting on the sofa.*

*She wears a dressing-gown. Her hair is unbrushed,
her face crumpled.*
BARBARA *is standing.*
They are two old women.

CAROLINE. You think he deserved it.

BARBARA *shakes her head.*

He tried to deserve it. It was his way of
committing suicide.

BARBARA *looks up, interested, but says nothing.*

Because what else is there to do? We're dying
out. If you're a pig you might as well cut your
own throat as run round the yard squealing.
Why did Laurence turn out so horrible? He was
promising. He had all the right ideas, you used
to think. But he lost touch. He lost his grip. He
wasn't just a right-wing bigot, he was a parody
of a right-wing bigot. Didn't you think so? Didn't
you think he rather overdid it? Or did you fall
for the whole thing? Did you really? Did you
never suspect? No? I thought you would, of all
people. You're not so bright as you and I think.
Sneering to yourself, poor Caroline, stuck with a
senile fascist. You really did? He was very good,
wasn't he, he could have been a great actor.
'This is pure parody, Laurence,' I would say.
'Nobody will believe a word of it.' He said,
'Don't worry Caroline. Anything I'm fool
enough to say, they'll be fool enough to believe.'
Even you. He had to make himself worse and
worse because at first we would think he was
shocking and next day we'd meet someone at
dinner saying far more stupid and aggressive
things. Unless they were pretending too of
course, unless every reactionary fool in the
country is playing at it, it may all be a vast plot.
Perhaps when we rode our ponies in Hyde Park,
two little girls with ringlets, we were pretending,
do you think so? We came home to tea and
mama's hands were cold and smooth. She was
never the one who cleaned the floors.

But why, you're about to ask me. Do you find you don't understand your Laurence quite so well? Some things he didn't have to pretend. He liked whisky, that came easily, and he despised you. He did despise your weak liberal slop just as he said. Because he might have been like you. He was. He didn't go to fight in Spain. He didn't have to leave the Communist Party over Hungary because he had never joined it. He lived on day after day. Then the crisis came. He couldn't sleep. Everyone in middle age wonders what on earth they've done with their life. Then they carry on. But he stopped. He lay there night after night. The oppressed people were rising all over the world he said and he found himself on the wrong side. And what could he do now? Could he extricate himself from his career, his large house, the money his father left him, the whisky? No, he had to admit, no. He was cut off forever from people who suffered. He had become the enemy. He loathed himself. He said he would commit suicide. And then at a brilliant stroke he saw what he could do for other people. He could be the enemy. He saw that violence was necessary but he couldn't have brought himself to be violent. Comfort makes the conscience tender. It had to be the oppressed who rose up and he could never be one of them. But he could help them to revolt by making them hate him. He could live out his way of life but more extremely. He could help make the establishment so despicable that everyone would see it had to go. He could use his power so unjustly that someone would be forced to take it away from him. He wouldn't kill but he could be killed. He could give his life for the revolution.

So what he had to do was make himself hated by everybody. Sometimes by me. It hasn't been easy. I can't say we've had a happy life. But that you see was what he was doing.

BARBARA. I don't believe you, Caroline. I think you're

making it up.

CAROLINE *doesn't react. She sits impassive,*
BARBARA *looking at her. A long silence.*

The JUDGE's *house from across the road, as before.*
The JUDGE *is leaving, going with* WARREN,
exactly as before, repeating the sequence ending with
the JUDGE *lying dead in the wood.*

THE AFTER-DINNER
JOKE

List of characters in order of appearance:

SELBY, a young woman
PRICE, an old man
POPSTAR, a man of maybe 30
MAYOR, a man of at least 45
CELEBRITY, a woman, any age
3 COUNCILLORS, men or women, any age
3+ FASTERS, men or women, fairly young
CHILDREN, various
3+ RECORD BREAKERS, various
SON, 9 to 11 years old
MUM, 30+
BRUCE WINGFIELD, a middle-aged man
THIEF, a young man
BABY
CUSTOMER, a man, any age
LICENSEE, a man, any age
MAN WITH JUBILEE MUG, middle-aged
COLLECTOR, a young man
WOMEN WITH SHOE, any age
ASSISTANT, a woman, any age
MAN WITH CAMERA or woman
WOMAN WITH CATALOGUE, over 50
OLD LADY
BUYER, needn't be a man
SALESMAN, likely to be a man
OIL SHEIKH, any age
WIVES, any age
BODYGUARDS, young enough to look strong
KNITTED-HAT LADY, at least 45
DENT, about 45
WOMAN, probably middle-aged
TEA MANAGING DIRECTOR, about 60
SIR ARTHUR, about 60
MOTHER, young
BABY
MAN, about 30
GIRL, 20s
COWBOYS, various
CHILD, any
AMERICAN PATIENT, 50 to 60 years old

ARAB GARDENER, a man, any age
VILLAIN, a man, any age
PEASANT, a man, any age
MINISTER, not under 40
PASSENGER, a man, 45 to 60 years old
GIRL, 20s
GUERRILLA, a man, any age except old
JOURNALIST, man or woman, any age
BUSINESSMEN, mainly middle-aged
PEASANTS, men or women, any age

The only parts of any size are SELBY, PRICE, MAYOR, DENT. The others can be doubled, trebled, quadrupled . . .

The After-Dinner Joke was first transmitted on BBC 1 on 14 February 1978, directed by Colin Bucksey. The cast was as follows:

SELBY	Paula Wilcox
PRICE	Richard Vernon
DENT	Clive Merrison
MAYOR	Derek Smith
BRUCE WINGFIELD	Ben Aris
PASSENGER	Philip Sayer
PATIENT	Hal Galili
GIRL	Heather Wright
JOURNALIST	Tom Georgeson
THIEF	George Innes
MINISTER	James Bree
CELEBRITY	Sheila Brennan
KNITTED HAT LADY	Patricia Lawrence
MUM	Sandy Ratcliff
UPPER-CLASS WOMAN	Julia McCarthy
WOMAN WITH CATALOGUE	Stella Moray
POP STAR	Peter Blake
TEA MANAGER	Raymond Francis
COLLECTOR	Lee Walker
MAN IN PUB	Richard Aylen
MERCHANT	Saeed Jaffrey
SHEIKH	Ishaq Bux
COWBOY	Luke Hanson

1

PRICE *and* SELBY.

PRICE *is sitting behind a large desk*; SELBY *is standing in front of it.*

PRICE.   Do I understand you're resigning, Miss Selby?

SELBY.   I want to do good, Mr Price.

PRICE.   And you think that being personal secretary to my sales manager isn't doing good?

SELBY.   No, sir.

PRICE.   Perhaps you think my sales manager isn't doing good?

SELBY.   It's just that I –

PRICE.   Perhaps you think the whole of Price's Bedding isn't doing good?

SELBY.   It's not, no.

PRICE.   And you think my department store doesn't do good?

SELBY.   No, it doesn't.

PRICE.   And I suppose my estate agents don't do good?

SELBY.   No.

PRICE.   And my launderettes and my chinese restaurants and my novelty factory making fireworks and crackers?

SELBY.   No.

PRICE.   I give employment. I provide services. I pay taxes. I make profits.

SELBY.   Children are dying, sir.

PRICE.   I see.

SELBY.   The cost of a six-foot Weldorm with

Slumberland mattress and headboard would buy a pump for a well and a camel cart and a –

PRICE.   Miss Selby, are you a Christian?

SELBY.   Not any more. But I feel just as guilty as if I was. And so should you.

PRICE.   Well done, Miss Selby, well done. When I was a young man and bought a penny doughnut for my tea, I always put a penny in the lifeboat stocking. And as I built up from my first little shop, my great joy has always been that I have given more and more to charity.

He gets out a bottle of whisky and two glasses and pours drinks as he talks.

I am on the boards of five charities. Two great charities I founded myself. And I will be happy to go on paying your salary, Miss Selby, while you work full time as one of our campaign organisers raising funds in towns throughout the country. Your health.

SELBY.   I don't usually like to drink, sir, because the cost of one glass of whisky would buy thirty trees to prevent soil erosion.

PRICE.   You can stop feeling guilty about world poverty, Miss Selby. You've started doing something about it.

SELBY.   Cheers.

She knocks back her drink.

2

A POPSTAR.

POPSTAR.   I said gimme

I said gimme what I need I said gimme
I said
gimme gimme gimme gimme gimme gimme
gimme gimme gimme

Cheers and screams.

Now that song is from two years back and I still
sing it because it still sells but it's not true now
I've discovered Jesus. I know now how to get
what I want. I do the opposite. Yes, that's right.
God moves in these mysterious ways. How you
get what you want is you give. If you give you're
needed. If you're needed you're loved. You
need to be needed. You need to be loved. That's
what you're after. That's what I'm after. Gimme
love. Now if you give, the people you give to are
going to love you. Jesus Christ is going to love
you. And I am going to love you.

Cheers and screams.

3

SELBY *and the* MAYOR.

A large wall-map of the town.

SELBY.   What I want to know, Mr Mayor, is where in
            your town the people with money are, so I can
            get it off them.

MAYOR.   You won't find it easy. They're all conservatives
            and won't play golf with me.

SELBY.   Where do they live?

MAYOR.   Up here on the hill.

SELBY.   And down here?

MAYOR.   Between the high street and the canal is what we
            call the old town.

SELBY.   The slums.

MAYOR.   The redevelopment area.

SELBY.   I just don't want to waste any leaflets. If you
            give me the population and housing statistics I
            can rule out the areas with multi-occupation.

MAYOR.   Just because the conservatives have more money
            that's no reason to think we in the labour
            movement aren't as generous as anyone else.
            Just because Ted Heath conducts Christmas
            carols –

SELBY.   No, I didn't mean to imply –

MAYOR.   and Margaret Thatcher supports Help the Aged
            and Prince Charles makes a jubilee appeal –

SELBY.   No, of course –

MAYOR.   Everyone thinks they're so kindhearted, and I'm
            every bit as kindhearted as they are, just because
            they're crowned heads, I'd be generous if I had
            a palace full of royal heritage and my mug on
            mugs, and a certain conservative councillor I can
            name keeps his wife on such a tight allowance
            she had to ask for an extra half-p when the
            postage went up so she could write to her lover –

SELBY.   No politics, please.

MAYOR.   I beg your pardon?

SELBY.   A charity is by definition nonpolitical. Politics is
            by definition uncharitable.

MAYOR.   But this poor lady is kept on a shoestring and
            charity begins at home, and this conservative
            councillor –

SELBY.   The royal family takes part in charity, so that
            just shows. Royalty is charitable. Royalty is
            nonpolitical. Therefore charity is nonpolitical.

MAYOR.   If I could take that again slowly. Royalty is
            charitable. Charity is nonpolitical. Therefore
            royalty is nonpolitical.

SELBY.   Do you doubt that?

MAYOR.   In a certain light everything is political.

SELBY.   There's nothing political at all about royalty.

MAYOR.   There's something political about everything.

SELBY.   Everything except royalty. And charities. What's political about royalty? Horses? Badminton horse trials, polo at Windsor, racing at Epsom? Or cars? Princess Anne breaking the speed limit? A jubilee parade of antique Rolls Royces? You're going to try and tell me that a queen and dukes and an honours list and men on the moor banging away at grouse and thousands of pounds' worth of shares that are undisclosed have something to do with politics, but that only goes to show how wrong you are.

MAYOR.   Are you interested in snakes at all?

SELBY.   No, not at all. I'm only interested in not wasting my valuable leaflets paid for by people who want to think every penny goes into powdered milk and blankets, silly buggers, how do they think they'd know about us if we didn't pay for advertising? No, I don't mean they're silly buggers, they're wonderful warmhearted folk, and I'm not wasting their valuable leaflets on unemployed nerks who won't give a good return for time and motion spent.

MAYOR.   That's a pity, because snakes are completely nonpolitical and I have a very interesting collection of pythons and boa constrictors and –

SELBY.   You get the odd old-age pensioner with pennies in the teapot and it's the thought that counts but widows' mites don't pay for wellbores, and I'm sure as a supporter of our charity you'd agree –

MAYOR.   I don't give that for your charity, to be honest. I'm only interested in my snakes. The largest python is nearly fifteen feet long. I sometimes go out at night in the springtime with a large sack and I have him on a special lead with a

harness I've made and I creep up to this field
with all the lambs and I open the sack and –

4

A CELEBRITY.

CELEBRITY. I've been asked to launch this charity
campaign because I'm a local celebrity and
everyone will think that if they give something
they'll be celebrities too. It's only charity
organisers who've ever actually called me a
celebrity, which certainly isn't the only reason I
support charities but because of their wonderful
work with the starving millions. Now I write a
cookery column and how lucky we are to have
delicious dishes even at today's prices compared
to the starving millions who have less calories in
one day than you have for breakfast, unless
you're one of those sillies who goes without
breakfast. Always always have a cooked
breakfast, even if you're on a diet, because – But
anyway in Ethiopia not so long ago people were
dying by the roadside and in Bangladesh many
people are lucky if they have a bowl of rice and
vegetables at a feeding station, and lucky they
are, because I have a recipe this week for
courgettes au gratin with saffron rice which you
just crisp up under the grill and – as I was
saying these poor people may have nothing in
the larder but a little pile of flour and a few
beans and, however good the recipe, ingredients
do make all the difference, so always use the
best butter, free-range eggs, double cream,
because no one in the Third
World is actually going to benefit by you eating
margarine, the only thing of course is watch the
cholesterol. But if you feel like spoiling yourself,
and in these days of inflation luxuries have

actually gone up less than necessities so it's economic sense to live well if you can, I have a recipe here where you wrap the smoked salmon round the –

5

Three COUNCILLORS *are sitting in a sideshow, with the labels* LIB, LAB, CON, *and people are paying 50p to throw pies at them. Splat. A custard pie is thrown in the face of a* COUNCILLOR. *They are keeping cheerful. Pies keep coming.*

VOICES.   (*In the crowd*). Nice to see them working together for once.

It's what this country needs to set it on its feet.

Daddy, what's lib lab con?

Well sweetheart, the Labour Party and the Liberal Party got together and that's known as the lib-lab con.

Don't they mind?

I expect they like the attention.

Splat, splat.

6

The MAYOR.

MAYOR.   – a large lump in the python which is the lamb it has swallowed whole, it's amazing how their throats open and their scales spread, and the python will lie still for a long time while the creature is gradually digested and not require any food for several weeks.

7

More sideshows.

A sponsored fast.
Some of the group are exhausted, others are squabbling.

1.   Sugar's cheating.

2.   No, it's not.

1.   Yes it is, we said liquids but no milk and sugar.

2.   Then why's it all right for you to drink orange juice?

3.   I've lost five pounds but I bet I put it all on again.

> *A sponsored silence.*
> *A group of children, all except one near bursting point from keeping quiet. Finally one starts to giggle, they all start, except the one, who goes on sitting silently.*
>
> *Sponsored record breakers.*
>
> *Various activities; e.g., a girl standing on her head, a boy playing a comb and tissue paper, a man eating doughnuts.*

8

A SON and his MUM.

SON.   I don't want to go on the sponsored walk.

MUM.   You got all those names.

SON.   I got a tummy-ache.

MUM.   How much you got a mile if you add it all up?

SON.   Eighty p.

MUM.   If you walk ten miles that's eight pounds.

SON.   Why can't they just give me the money?

MUM.   You have to earn it. People won't give money
            for nothing.

SON.   It doesn't do them any good if I walk does it?

MUM.   It's good for you.

SON.   I got a tummy-ache.

MUM.   It's fresh air.

SON.   If they want to give the money, I don't see why
            they can't just give it, I don't see why I have to
            walk round and round the park all afternoon, I
            want to play football and watch telly, why can't
            they sponsor me to watch telly, I'd do that for
            hours, they'd get far more out of me, I don't see
            how it's going to help some hungry person in
            Africa if I walk round and round the park all
            afternoon with a tummy-ache and get blisters
            and –

MUM.   All right, I'll buy you training shoes, now stop
            going on.

SON.   Will you, Mum? Now? Now will you? For this
            afternoon?

MUM.   All right, I said I will, now give over.

SON.   They're really good, Mum, everyone's got them
            and they're only seven ninety-five and I'll walk
            ten miles in them easy, well nine or ten.

9

The MAYOR.

MAYOR.   Snakes aren't slimy. People think they are. They
            don't feel like frogs. They're really very pleasant
            to the touch.

10

SELBY *and* BRUCE WINGFIELD.

BRUCE *is practising golf shots with a fixed ball on his lawn.*

BRUCE.   I already give a great deal to charity.

SELBY.   Which charities do you give to?

BRUCE.   There's one to support Eton College and one to support the London Clinic and one –

SELBY.   But those are charities that help the rich. I thought charities had to help the poor.

BRUCE.   Are you getting political?

SELBY.   No no no.

BRUCE.   They are very old, established charities set up to provide education and hospital care.

SELBY.   But the government provides those nowadays.

BRUCE.   The government also provides foreign aid.

SELBY.   Ah but charities though small go direct to the people, bypassing all governments whatever their politics, and set up different schemes the government hasn't covered and –

BRUCE.   Exactly, and I've found something the government hasn't covered and I'm setting up a charity to benefit company directors called Bruce Wingfield, five foot ten, brown hair, living in Englefield Avenue, and playing golf.

SELBY.   Would you be a beneficiary of this charity?

BRUCE.   As it happens, yes, I would.

SELBY.   You can't do that. It has to be a broader category. The charity commissioners would never allow it.

BRUCE.   Are you quite sure?

SELBY. Almost.

BRUCE. Perhaps if I make it company directors called *Bruce*, five foot ten *to eleven*, brown *or mousy* hair, living in Englefield Avenue *or Gardens*. And playing golf.

SELBY. You've already got a two-car garage.

BRUCE. Are you getting political?

SELBY. No no no no no, I'm not getting political, no –

11

The COUNCILLORS; *a* THIEF.

Splat. Another pie. The COUNCILLORS *are trying to look as if they're still enjoying it.*
In the crowd, a THIEF *picks a pocket.*

12

A MUM *and her* BABY.

MUM. Eat up for Mummy.

BABY. No.

MUM. Just a spoonful for Mummy.

BABY. No.

MUM. Spoonful for Daddy.

BABY. No.

MUM. Spoonful for Nan.

BABY. No.

MUM. Spoonful for Batman.

The BABY *opens his mouth and has some. Then spits it out.*

Batman's going to be very cross with you. Batman won't let you be Robin. Batman's going to give you to the Joker and he'll put you in a machine that'll take all your brains away and you'll be a vegetable, you'll be a plate of gooey green spinach yourself.

MUM *calms herself and starts again.*

Open your mouth. Doggy's going to get it. Doggy wants your dindin. Open quick. Mummy give dindin to doggy. Look there's thousands of people would like this dinner, right? There's millions of Indians want this dinner. This is your last chance, right? Right. I'm sending it to India. Everything. Yes even your sweeties, bad boys don't get sweeties.

MUM *puts the food from the table and fridge into a carrier bag.*

Sweeties go to India, eggies go to India, crispy cod fries go to India, crinkle cut chips go to India, prawn curry goes to India, raspberry ripple ice cream goes to India, fizzy orange goes to India, you sodding go to India.

MUM *puts the bag over the* BABY's *head.*

13

SELBY, *a* CUSTOMER *and a* LICENSEE.

SELBY.   Twenty pence would vaccinate a child against measles, fifty pence would buy eighty trees to prevent soil erosion, one pound would buy eight feet of waterpipe, five pounds would buy a pig.

An off-licence.

CUSTOMER. Bottle of whisky, please.

LICENSEE. Here you are, sir.

> *The* LICENSEE *gives the* CUSTOMER *a pig.*

14

Stock film of a sponsored walk.

15

The MAYOR *and* SELBY.

MAYOR.   I challenge you to tell me something apart from my snakes that is not political.

SELBY.   Anything. Just look about you. Say – anything.

MAYOR.   Say something.

SELBY.   House. No, wait a minute, not a house. Car. No, not a car. Tree. Tree.

MAYOR.   Tree. Timber. Price of. Building industry. Need I say more?

SELBY.   Rain.

MAYOR.   Rain. Leaks. Section 99 of the Public Health Act calling for repairs to substandard housing. The number of prosecutions in this town last year –

SELBY.   Fish. No no no, not fish. Not fish. Not cow. Haha, butter mountain. No farm animals. Wildebeest.

MAYOR.   A wildebeest is a South African animal.

SELBY .   Not a wildebeest, no, I didn't say wildebeest. I said butterfly. That's it, butterfly. Butterfly,

summer day, blue sky, flowers, long grass,
strolling through the long grass with a nice
bloke and finding a place to sit down among all
the flowers and butterflies.

16

A MAN with a jubilee mug and a COLLECTOR with long hair.

MAN.   Give money to blacks?

COLLECTOR. Yeh well I mean like they're dying man.

MAN.   If I give them money they'll recover and land on
            the Sussex coast at dead of night and come and
            live next door.

COLLECTOR. No, if you don't give they'll get angry and all
            the ones that haven't died will get the atom
            bomb from Russia and drop it on you.

MAN.   Really?

COLLECTOR. Yeh.

MAN.   What if I do give then?

COLLECTOR. Then they'll be very grateful and stay where
            they belong and take O level English Literature
            and buy all our exports and wish they were still
            in the Empire and remember you in their
            prayers and think you're great, man.

MAN.   Really?

COLLECTOR. Yeh.

MAN.   Oh all right, here you are.

            He puts money in the collecting-box.

17

The MAYOR.

MAYOR.   Butterfly. Not so many about. Industrial
           pollution.

18

A WOMAN *with a shoe, and an* ASSISTANT.

WOMAN.   Have you got these in a five?

ASSISTANT. Here you are.

                She drags out a fishing boat.

19

A MAN *with a camera; a* THIEF.

The MAN *is taking pictures of the sponsored record breakers. He
puts the camera down on a seat beside him for a moment. The*
THIEF *takes it.*

20

A WOMAN *with a catalogue,* SELBY *and an* OLD LADY.

WOMAN.   We've adopted a granny.

SELBY.   That's wonderful.

WOMAN.   We had a catalogue from your company and we
         chose one. We'll get a grandpa next year to
         match.

SELBY.   Which one did you choose?

         The WOMAN *shows the photographs in the*
         catalogue.

WOMAN.   We asked for this one which was advertised, it
         says ninety-two and never a day of ill health,
         always cheerful – well, compared to my mother,
         I can tell you. But she'd already gone so they
         sent us another model, she's eighty-one and has
         suffered from leprosy for many years so that she
         has no fingers, but you can't catch it at this
         distance, and she sends us the nicest letters
         telling us how grateful she is and how wonderful
         we are, which is more than my mother ever did.

SELBY.   Is your mother dead?

WOMAN.   Oh no, I don't think so. We keep her in the
         corner. You don't want to get her noticing, you
         don't want to set her off talking, she's not at all
         a nice old lady.

         SELBY *reaches out to touch the* OLD LADY's
         shoulder. The OLD LADY *bites her hand.*

21

The COUNCILLORS; SELBY.

The COUNCILLORS *are finishing cleaning themselves up.*

LIB.   We made nearly fifty pounds.

CON.   I'd rather have written a cheque for fifty
         pounds.

LAB.   Most of the pies were thrown at me.

CON.   Yes, I reckon it's the equivalent of a 20 per cent swing.

LAB.   They naturally throw pies at the one in power. It shows respect.

LIB.   They threw quite a lot at me.

CON.   Never had so much notice taken of you.

LAB.   It's by association with me.

LIB.   Oh look. There's one pie left.

            LIB *edges towards the pie.*

LAB.   No, Harry.

CON.   Not when we've just got washed.

LAB.   We are on the same side.

CON.   I was hoping you'd join me for dinner.

            SELBY *comes in.*

SELBY.   I'd just like to thank you all so much for –

            Splat: Pie in SELBY's *face.*

22

The THIEF *climbs in through a window.*

23

SELBY *and the* MAYOR.

SELBY.   Sunset.

MAYOR.   Sunset. Romance.

SELBY.   Romance, there you are.

MAYOR.   Sunset. Romance. Marriage. Housework. Wages
            for Housework. We're getting into a whole area
            here –

SELBY.   Don't bother.

MAYOR.   Sex Discrimination Act. Equal pay.

SELBY.   I didn't mean sunset. Not sun*set*. Sunrise.

MAYOR.   Sun*rise*?

SELBY.   Yes.

MAYOR.   Rising sun?

SELBY.   That's right.

MAYOR.   Land of the rising sun? Japan? Rate of growth?

SELBY.   Not so much sun*rise*. Just sun.

MAYOR.   *Sun*. Newspaper.

SELBY.   No no, sun in the sky.

MAYOR.   Sun.

SELBY.   Sun.

24

A BUYER *and a* CAR SALESMAN.

BUYER.   When can I have delivery of this model?

SALESMAN. Right away sir.

            Enter fifty calves.

25

The POPSTAR *and* SELBY.

They are sharing a joint in the front of the POPSTAR's *parked car, while young girls swarm at the windows and on the bonnet.*

POPSTAR.　I really fancy girls about ten or twelve years old and they besiege me, they get in the car somehow – I expect there's one in the back now but I can't be bothered to turn round – I book into a hotel room and there's one waiting, but I reckon Jesus understands that because all you need is love isn't it, or it used to be a few years back, but now I find I need fast cars as well.

SELBY.　I do want to be liked. You're right there. It's not a good feeling that a whole lot of people round the world might be hating you. When I started this job, it was such a relief. But now unless I raise more and more each time I feel as bad as before I started. I don't know if this appeal's done any good.

POPSTAR.　It can't do my sales any harm. Whether it does any good to – what is it this time? Starving Bangladeshis it was a few years back, and Ethiopia's not in the charts now but these things are always with us, and I really do envy your job, it's the only thing I'd like to do except be a really great rock star. I mean love and starvation are two of the basics. And fast cars.

26

An OIL SHEIKH, *his* VEILED WIVES *and their* BODYGUARDS.

Marks and Spencer's. The WIVES *are picking up armfuls of clothes and giving them to the* BODYGUARDS, *who are holding piles of clothes.*

SHEIKH.　(*in Arabic*). Stop.

　　　They stop.

(*In English*). This is a waste of time. I will buy
everything. All the sweaters. All the shirts. All
the underwear. The whole shop. All the shop
assistants. The whole building.

SELBY *and the* MAYOR.

MAYOR.   An Arab oil sheikh has just bought Marks and
Spencer's. He's having it taken down and
shipped brick by brick back to the desert.

SELBY.   Quick, he might give something.

MAYOR.   I wonder if he'd like to take the town hall. I
could start collecting scorpions.

The SHEIKH *and* SELBY.

The SHEIKH *takes bundles of notes from under his
robe and gives them to* SELBY.

SHEIKH.   For the poor English.

A VOICE *over stills.*

VOICE.   Camels have been replaced by Cadillacs in
Kuwait which brings smiles to the inhabitants of
Kensington and ·Chelsea as they receive their
first gifts of discarded camels.

A still of English people with a camel.

Strikers at a midland car factory who would like
to be adopted by an Arab family.

A still of strikers.

Bales of clothing have been opened and
distributed, bringing delight to this old
Englishman.

*A rapid series of stills of an old Englishman taking off
his clothes and struggling into Arab robes.*

27

PRICE *and* SELBY.

PRICE.   Well done, Miss Selby, well done. That's the
           largest sum ever collected in one town and
           makes you regional organiser of the year with
           your picture in our newsletter. I'd like you to
           attend my next business lunch where I persuade
           as many businessmen as possible to involve their
           companies in charity work and I'd like you to
           learn all about tax concessions so you can talk to
           them. And then I'd like to promote you to the
           publicity department of our central office.

28

A LADY *in a knitted hat*; DENT.

DENT.   (*voice*). A message from the publicity
           department.

LADY.   People think charities are just ladies in knitted
           hats with nothing better to do, very amateurish
           and muddled but full of warmth and
           compassion. Well I work for this charity and
           that is exactly what I'm like but the charity itself
           is extremely businesslike and professional and
           commercial.

DENT.   People think charities these days are too
           businesslike and professional and commercial.
           Well I work for this charity and that is exactly
           what I'm like but the charity itself is full of
           warmth and compassion and we have all these
           wonderful ladies in knitted hats.

29

The THIEF *robs a bank.*

30

The MAYOR *and* SELBY.

MAYOR.   Sun. Drought. Starvation.

SELBY.   That's not political. It's an act of God.

31

DENT, SELBY *and* PRICE.

SELBY *is writing at a desk.* DENT *is restless.*

DENT.   We'll have Price here in a minute yattering on about his doughnuts. I hope you've learnt in your time with me that a charity has to be run like any other business. It exists to make money. Mr Price can talk about Christian brotherhood and the joy of giving, and it's men of vision like him who get things started. But once you get into the day to day, what matters is the figures at the bottom of the columns. Whether to buy the freehold of the gift shops. Whether to leave our latest bequest in Imperial Tobacco. The sooner we can get rid of him and get on with some real work – good afternoon, Mr Price, nice to see you.

PRICE *comes in.*

PRICE.   Ah Miss Selby. Hard at it as usual. You remind

me of myself at your age when I used to go out
and buy a doughnut and always put a penny –

DENT.   Miss Selby's working on some ideas for our next
           publicity campaign.

PRICE.   Good, let's hear them.

DENT.   I haven't looked at them myself yet. It might
           save time if you –

PRICE.   It doesn't matter if they're not good. It's the
           spirit in which she does it that matters.

DENT.   By the time of your next visit we could select –

PRICE.   I want to know what goes on in everyone's head.
           Are you trying to keep me out of my own
           charity? The baker never interfered.

DENT.   What we're trying to do is get a hardhitting
           dynamic campaign that is acceptable to the
           public. Oxfam devised a commercial showing a
           cake with a white hand cutting a slice and then
           taking the whole cake and a black hand taking
           the slice. We want to avoid anything like that.

PRICE.   It sounds rather clever.

DENT.   It was clever. It was accurate. It was hardhitting.
           ITV wouldn't show it. They said it was political.

PRICE.   Oh well. Political. Of course we don't want to be
           political. Suppose we had a cake and . . . oh well.
           Let's listen to Miss Selby.

SELBY.   I thought a picture of a dead child. You can see
           its ribs sticking out, its swollen stomach, clearly it
           starved to death. Or a child that died of an
           illness, say measles, it could be covered with
           sores, whatever you like, this is a rough draft,
           you get the idea. And the caption: 'This is your
           fault.'

DENT.   No.

PRICE.   It's quite hardhitting, you know.

DENT.   It's out of the question. People don't like to be
           blamed.

SELBY.   You could have a dead child, and the caption: 'Whose fault is this?'

DENT.   There can never be any suggestion of fault.

SELBY.   Just a picture of a dead child?

DENT.   No no no.

PRICE.   She's doing her best. It's very good for a first try, Miss Selby. I came up with something like it once myself.

DENT.   Look, Miss Selby, people don't like to be made miserable. If your advertisement makes them feel bad, they'll put it out of their minds as fast as they can. You want something that makes them feel good. And makes them feel even better when they give the money.

SELBY.   An advertisement about people starving that's going to make people feel good?

DENT.   Exactly.

PRICE.   It is rather a tricky one.

DENT.   Perhaps by the next time you come –

PRICE.   Oh I don't mind waiting. I'm enjoying myself.

DENT.   If you'll excuse me, I'll just be –

SELBY.   I've got it. I've got it. A picture of a well-fed, smiling child and the caption: 'Who makes her happy?'

DENT.   That is more like it.

PRICE.   I knew she could do it.

SELBY.   It implies, you see, that you made her happy by giving her money and you feel good and so you do go and give some money because otherwise you won't feel quite so good and when you've given it you feel very good indeed.

DENT.   Congratulations, Miss Selby.

SELBY.   Well that's a relief. You had me worried there

for a moment. That's my first idea okayed. Now
this is my second idea. It's about coffee.

DENT.   Oxfam tried that. People don't like –

SELBY.   Wait till you hear this. A cup of coffee, you see,
and the caption, Does coffee cost too much?
And the reader thinks yes yes, it costs me a
pound a quarter, or whatever it is by the time
this is printed, you've got him on your side.
Then you let him have it: You can afford coffee
even at this high price but the people who pick
it can't. What does it cost them in suffering?
The extra money you pay isn't all going in
wages to coffee-bean pickers, don't you think it,
why have coffee share prices rocketed, and tea
the same – we'd have a similar one about tea –
the conditions people who pick tea live in would
spoil your tea party if you saw them, oh yes, and
a certain tea company who shall be nameless –
or we might name them – made twice the profits
this year they did last year, and it all started
because Britain was a colonial power and made
people in those countries grow tea and coffee
for you to drink instead of food for themselves,
and sugar too, you may think sugar's gone up,
my God, do you read the business pages of your
newspaper, the eyes of the sugar world are on
the talks between the EEC and the sugar-
producing countries, and the EEC doesn't want
to give them the 4 per cent increase they're
asking and you have the nerve to complain
about immigration when they come here looking
for a better standard of living and I hope you
feel pretty sick every time you drink a cup of tea
or coffee and put sugar in it and think where it
comes from and give a whole lot of money to
charity because you're no better than slave
dealers and you're not drinking tea and coffee
you're drinking human blood, sweat and tears.

PRICE.   That's jolly good. Perhaps a little bit strong.

SELBY.   It doesn't have to be in exactly those words, of

course. We'd polish it up. I'm more than happy
to rewrite it.

DENT.   Wouldn't you say it was a little bit political?

PRICE.   Was it, Miss Selby? Oh dear. That's not what I
          expected of you at all. You always seem such a
          nice girl.

SELBY.   Political? Oh no no no no no. I wouldn't dream.
          No. Political? Ha ha, good heavens, no no. No.

32

A WOMAN.

WOMAN.   Dear sir, I have given to your charity for many
          years but I will demand my money back if there
          are any more disgusting appeals blaming me for
          the state of the world. I don't mind being told a
          rich person has a duty to give crumbs off his
          plate to the poor man at the gate, but I won't
          stand for being told I'm wrong to be rich,
          especially when I'm not. I particularly resent in
          Jubilee year any suggestion that Britannia
          doesn't play fair. Anyone would think from your
          appeal that these people have some right to a
          fair share of the world's resources. Next I
          suppose you'll be suggesting they needn't say
          thank you.

33

DENT, SELBY *and* PRICE.

DENT.   If you want to be political, Miss Selby –

SELBY.   No no no –

DENT.   If you want to suggest that there are causes of world poverty and they are to be found largely in our systems of trade and government, there are magazines that put this point of view. We contribute to the financing of these magazines but completely dissociate ourselves from what they say.

SELBY.   Yes yes yes, I do dissociate –

PRICE.   I'm sure her heart is in the right place.

DENT.   In this way we help spread the idea to the few people who may be receptive to it and get the more subversive young people out of the charity itself, where they're a terrible nuisance because they're the same types who want workers' control and a place on the board, when what we need is all the titles and captains of industry we can get, so as I say we get rid of them to these magazines and keep our own image of a completely nonpolitical charity spreading a little sunshine.

SELBY.   No no, I want to work for the charity. I just got carried away by the facts. I did have this third idea, I don't expect you want to hear it, it is hardhitting, well we could polish it up. I thought – it's just an idea – well what it is . . . is a big poster with big red letters saying Fuck you, greedy pigs – no. No no no no no. Just off the top of my head. An idea. No. Haha. No.

DENT.   Oxfam are selling this little book. It's a collection of after dinner stories called *Pass the Port*. It's 'a glittering array of famous people parting with gems of wit usually reserved for their intimate friends.' It's 'what royalty, a prime minister, judges, bishops, trade union leaders, admirals, senior academics, and captains of industry consider to be funny in our day.' After dinner jokes by top people. That's far more the spirit.

34

The MANAGING DIRECTOR *of a tea company.*

TEA MAN.   You may at this very moment be drinking a cup
of our tea. It has been alleged that my company
made twice as much profit this year as last year.
In fact we made twice as much profit this year
as last year. But really you know the conditions
of our tea pickers aren't so abysmally frightful as
when people first started criticising us. We've
improved their conditions so they are now only
as frightful as those of people doing similar
work in these countries. It would be ridiculous
to expect us to raise their wages to anything
approaching yours, although of course we'd love
to do that, because they would then be far better
off than their neighbours. I hope you'll feel
better about our tea when you think that not
just the tea pickers but everyone in those
countries is living in what you would consider
for your own family to be appalling destitution –
everyone of that class, I should say, because
there are of course people in every country of
the free world who are enormously rich, just as
there are in this country.

35

The THIEF *running along the roof of a train.*

36

DENT.

DENT.   I have been under attack for the way I run our
gift shops. These shops sell goods made in poor

– sorry, underdeveloped, sorry, developing –
countries, providing a livelihood for the
craftsmen, cheap gifts for you and a profit for
us to put back into the charity. It has been
suggested we are taking too much profit but we
are paying the workers a more than fair wage in
terms of their own country. It's because labour is
so cheap there that we are able to sell the goods
cheap to you and if they weren't cheap you
wouldn't buy them. A charity is a business and
the profits are put to good use and we can't
raise their living standards to anything
approaching yours because – and anyway we're
only talking about a tiny fraction of the
population, do you think charities deal in large
sums of money, England spends as much on
defence in a year as all the rich countries
together spend on aid, and aid is massive
compared to charity, what are we talking about?
We sell hanging baskets made of jute from
Bangladesh. Britain has frozen jute out of our
markets. What's a few thousand hanging
baskets? So there's no need at all to get at me
for the way I run our gift shops.

37

The MAYOR *and* SELBY.

MAYOR.   Sun?

SELBY.   Sun.

MAYOR.   Sun, moon, planets, space programme, cost of.

SELBY.   That's American politics.

MAYOR.   Sun, heat, alternative source of energy, you see
         where we're getting, dangers of nuclear power,
         Windscale fast breeder, future of coal industry –
         Or again, sun, Spain, holidays, rate of exchange –

SELBY.   All right, all right.

MAYOR.   My snakes aren't political at all.

38

The THIEF *kidnaps* SIR ARTHUR *at gunpoint into a car.*

39

SELBY, PRICE *and* DENT.

SELBY.   Nobody sells cigarettes. Or margarine. Or
            breakfast cereal. They sell getting more girls or
            pleasing your man or being a good mum. We're
            too direct, selling poor countries. We must sell
            what people want. All right, they want to feel
            good about the starving millions, but there's
            plenty of things they want more than that.

PRICE.   But charity is more spiritual than margarine.

DENT.   Charity is business. You're a businessman, Mr
            Price.

PRICE.   Yes, I've tried to run my business with an eye to
            charity.

DENT.   And your charity with an eye to business. Charity
            is inseparable from capitalism.

40

A MOTHER *and her* BABY.

The MOTHER *is holding the* BABY, *who puts a coin in a
collecting-box.*

VOICE.   Build a safe world – for him.

41

A MAN *and a* GIRL.

The MAN *puts a necklace round the* GIRL'*s neck, then writes a cheque while she leans over admiringly.*

VOICE.   When you want to give her the world, give to her
              favourite charity.

42

COWBOYS; *a* CHILD.

The COWBOYS *shoot it out.*

A lone survivor walks out. He sees a CHILD *with a begging bowl. He tosses money into it.*

VOICE.   A man's gotta do what a man's gotta do – give.

43

The THIEF, SIR ARTHUR *and* SELBY.

The THIEF *and* SIR ARTHUR *are in a bare room.*
The THIEF *and* SELBY *talk through the locked door.*

SELBY. I'm not armed.

THIEF. Twenty thousand, five hundred and ninety-six pounds I've got for you already. That's the train robbery, the bank robbery and various odds and ends. And when they pay the ransom you'll have another half million.

SELBY. That's very kind of you.

THIEF. Think what it's going to buy. Wells. Tractors. Eye operations.

SELBY. But we can't accept money got by crime.

THIEF. Crime? Whose crime? Isn't it their crime having it when people are starving?

SELBY. Yes but –

THIEF. You don't deny that Robin Hood is a folk hero?

SELBY. No but –

THIEF. Then whose side are you on?

SELBY. But people have to give the money themselves because they want to or it's not charity.

THIEF. Look, the reason I went into this. I've got friends who do the same thing but in their case for political motives. They rob banks for liberation movements. But I'm a pacifist. I don't want the money I steal spent on guns. I'd rather have it spent on medicines. I'd rather give it to poor farmers to buy equipment. I'm aiming to personally redistribute the wealth of the world.

SELBY. Singlehanded?

THIEF. If I devote my whole life to it. And other people will follow my example. Are you trying to put me down for only having half a million pounds? It's going to add up.

SELBY. There's quite a lot of money to be shifted.

THIEF. You tell me who's ever given half a million to your charity. If everyone who gives 50p now raised half a million we'd be getting somewhere. I reckon in about fifty years the world will be transformed.

SELBY. But what about all the governments and . . . You can't transform the world just by getting money from individuals.

THIEF. Then what are you in a charity for? You sound like my friends in liberation. But I don't agree. I believe in charities. If every man, woman and child in the western world stole a thousand pounds a year –

SELBY. I think you should consider letting Sir Arthur go.

THIEF. Unilever invests as much in Africa in a couple of days as you raise in a whole year. You're like kids spending pocket money. So what are you going to do about it?

SELBY. We accept that we can do very little.

THIEF. You do?

SELBY. Yes.

THIEF. You help a few hundred people out of millions and you accept that?

SELBY. What else can we do if that's all people give?

THIEF. You take it from them.

SELBY. Not by stealing it.

THIEF. How else? I'm not interested in politics. I believe in charities. If his company doesn't pay the ransom by midnight I'm going to shoot him. And if your charity doesn't accept the money I'm going to shoot him. And if you stand out there saying stupid things I'm going to shoot you. So think about it.

44

The MAYOR.

MAYOR.   A favourite pet of mine is the rubber boa, a small
            snake perhaps twenty inches long, whose tail
            looks very much like its head. When it meets an
            enemy it curls up in a ball and sticks out its tail
            and waves it about so it looks like the head of a
            striking snake. If the enemy attacks the tail, the
            rubber boa brings out its head and bites it.
            They're not normally aggressive though so they
            make a good pet, the only trouble is, being a
            burrowing snake, he's usually under the earth in
            his pen and I don't see as much of him as I would
            like.

45

DENT, SELBY *and* PRICE.

DENT.   It's most important not to come to the end of the
            financial year with too large a balance or people
            will think we don't know what to do with the
            money.

SELBY.   What are we going to do with the money?

DENT.   That's what we don't know.

PRICE.   I never remember why that's a problem. Can't we
            just send Miss Selby with a big bag of notes and
            she could walk about handing them to the poor
            people. I'd go myself if I was younger. Oh I'd
            love to do that and see their happy faces.

DENT.   It's a bit more complicated than that.

PRICE.   Yes, to be fair we should share it out equally. Just
            to give me an idea, what would one million
            pounds come to divided among the most

destitute people in the world, not including everyone worse off than us, but the ones we can really hardly bear to imagine, just as a rough estimate for planning purposes?

DENT.   Roughly one thousandth of a penny each.

PRICE.   Well. I'll have to resign myself yet again to not being able to help everyone. But even one life saved, one person made happy, has its value. Perhaps we should make it simple and Miss Selby should go out to India or Africa or South America and the first person she meets give him the whole million. That would at least make one very happy Indian.

DENT.   When I say we don't know what to do with the money I don't mean we don't know what to do with the money.

SELBY.   Of course not.

DENT.   We have plenty of agents and field-workers looking for the best possible projects. But what with the sheikh and the commercials and Sir Arthur's legacy we have a greater surplus than usual and I'd like to find some really special use for it.

PRICE.   The sheikh has just built a large hospital in the desert. Why don't we send Miss Selby out to get some ideas?

46

An AMERICAN PATIENT, SELBY *and an* ARAB GARDENER.

The PATIENT *is in a wheelchair in a flowery garden.*
The GARDENER *stands hosing the lawn.*

PATIENT. When I had a heart attack I thought the end had come. I was frightened even to cut my finger in this country. There's people dying of disease everywhere, no sanitation, no doctors, nothing. But we radioed for help and a helicopter brought me two hundred miles to the hospital. And it's just great. I've got a private room, pretty nurses, vases of flowers from this wonderful garden. If I wanted a heart transplant they could do it, that's how good this hospital is.

SELBY. I suppose people come here from all over the place?

PATIENT. There's a woman flew a thousand miles to have her nose shortened. It has real international prestige.

SELBY. And anyone who's ill in any of the villages in the country, they come here?

PATIENT. If they can get here, sure. If you've no transport and you're feeling sick, I guess not too many of them bother.

SELBY. You mean most of the people are getting no medical treatment at all?

PATIENT. I guess not. But you have to set that against the fact that the treatment provided here is of the very highest quality. Just as this garden blooms in the desert on account of they have hoses playing on the lawn day and night.

SELBY. And outside the gate it's clouds of dust blowing about.

PATIENT. That's right. Isn't it great?

SELBY. It's not so great if you live outside the gate.

PATIENT. Yes, it's a very unfortunate thing there's no piped water in the villages. I've got some wonderful photographs of the women carrying big jars on their heads. I guess you'd say the men should carry it on their heads too. But some of the men get to work in the garden.

SELBY. For the money they've spent on this hospital they could have some sort of medical worker in every village.

PATIENT.   Sure, and what's a medical worker? I wouldn't
           want some highschool kid looking after me, and
           why should they? This hospital has some of the
           richest patients in the world, and they want the
           best just like we do in the west. You can't have
           heart transplants in every village. I can tell you I
           wouldn't be alive today if it wasn't for this hospital.

SELBY.   Yes but hundreds of people die in this country
           who never –

PATIENT.   Are you saying it doesn't matter whether or not I
           am alive today?

SELBY.   No but –

PATIENT.   What's the matter with you anyway? This hospital
           cures sick people and makes a damn good job of
           it. OK?

47

DENT *and* SELBY.

They are talking to each other on the phone.

DENT.   It doesn't make sense to give money to a country
           that's far richer than Britain even if the people
           are poorer. Well we do, I can think of examples,
           but not an oil state, really.

SELBY.   Then we must make the sheikh share out the
           money to the benefit of the people. Is there no
           one trying to do that already? There must surely
           be groups of people in the country who want the
           wealth to be in the hands of – sorry.

DENT.   They're called guerrillas.

SELBY.   Sorry.

DENT.   In Oman the British Army is fighting –

SELBY.   Look I'm not trying to be political, I'm trying to
           be sensible. I don't know why I keep –

DENT.   All right, we'll say no more about it. Go to a
         different country. Go somewhere unquestionably
         poor. Go to Bangladesh. Even with all the aid
         that's been poured in it's still full of hungry
         people. Straightforward need.

48

A VILLAIN *and a* PEASANT.

A silent movie of A Year in Bangladesh: *mime, captions, music.
The* VILLAIN *has the top hat and moustache of melodrama. The*
PEASANT *is in rags.*

1.   **The Landlord**

           The VILLAIN *demands the rent. The* PEASANT
           gives him sacks.
           Caption: 'Here's the rent, sir, half my grain.'

2.   **The Moneylender**

           The same VILLAIN, *this time as a moneylender sitting
           at a table with bags of money. The* PEASANT *is
           pleading with him.*
           *Captions: 'We've eaten our half of the grain. Can you
           lend me some money until the harvest?'*
           'Certainly. The interest is 200%.'

3.   **The Merchant at Harvest Time**

           The same VILLAIN, *this time as a merchant. The*
           PEASANT *with sacks.*
           *Captions: 'It's been a good harvest. If I sell nearly all
           my crop I can pay my debt.'*
           'Everyone's selling. The price is very low.'

4.   **The Merchant Six Months Later**

           The VILLAIN *as before. The* PEASANT *with a little
           money.*
           *Captions: 'I've no food left for my family. I want to buy
           some.'*

'Everyone's buying. The price has doubled.'

5. **The Landlord Again**

The distraught PEASANT *on his knees before the* VILLAIN.
Caption: 'If you can't pay the rent you'll be evicted.'

6. **The Charity**

The PEASANT *with a begging bowl.*

49

SELBY, *on the phone.*

SELBY. You know I recommended we buy boats for the
        fishermen . . . Well, there is a bit of bother,
        yes . . I am getting on with it, I'm getting round
        to it. You know the fishermen used to rent boats
        from these rich boat-owners who charged them
        so much and . . . Last night the boat-owners
        smashed up the boats. Not their boats, the
        fishermen's boats. Our boats . . . Rented the boat-
        owners' boats of course and gone fishing . . . Yes,
        that's what I'm doing, finding another project,
        yes.

50

The LADY *in the knitted hat.*

LADY.   A message from the publicity department.
        We have a wonderful charity gift shop in
        Johannesburg which is great fun and highly
        successful. The variety of things sold is almost as
        astounding as the variety of customers, some of

them hard-pressed blacks looking for cheap clothes, others arriving in Jags in the hope of finding antiques.

51

A MINISTER.

MINISTER. I have just come from the North-South conference between the rich and poor countries. And I've come to reassure you that we are not going to give them anything like what they are asking for. We are not going to wipe out their debts nor finance a common fund to stabilise their export prices. On the other hand, we are going to cancel some of their debts and give a little support to some kind of fund, because if we let these countries get too poor they won't be able to buy our goods, with disastrous effects on our own economy. Also the oil-producing countries are eager for us to help their less fortunate brothers. If we don't they might not sell us oil at a price we can afford to pay. Nobody likes to see millions of people living in misery, and I won't lose any votes if I tell you we are going to help them just enough to help ourselves.

52

The LADY *in the knitted hat.*

LADY.   A message from the publicity department.

A still of two old black women; her voice over.

These poor old ladies live not only on a rubbish
dump but in a very violent area. When our
photographer took this picture he narrowly
escaped having his camera smashed by young
troublemakers throwing stones. But the old
ladies somehow survive without being attacked.

53

A film of a hurricane.

54

DENT *and* PRICE.

DENT.   I thought we were never going to get the money
           spent. Miss Selby seems to be incapable of
           recommending a project. But now, thank God,
           we can transfer it to the hurricane disaster fund.

PRICE.   Yes, God seems to have solved the problem for
           us. We'll send Miss Selby straight to the scene of
           the disaster.

55

SELBY *and another* PASSENGER *on a plane.*

PASSENGER. You worried by takeoff?

SELBY.   Not very.

PASSENGER. Landing's worse.

SELBY.   Yes.

PASSENGER. Especially if there's no landing strip.

SELBY.   No landing strip?

PASSENGER. I imagine it's been blown away, Or buried under ten feet of mud. Or scattered all over with uprooted trees.

SELBY.   The control tower would tell the pilot.

PASSENGER. You think so?

SELBY.   You think not?

PASSENGER. Well it doesn't bother me, because the hazards of takeoff and landing are nothing to the journey itself. It's just starting to get dangerous now.

SELBY.   It says we can undo our seat-belts.

PASSENGER. Hi-jackers.

SELBY.   What? Where?

PASSENGER. I carry a cyanide capsule.

SELBY.   What? Why?

PASSENGER. You see people get up. You think they're just going to the bathroom. But suddenly one of them pulls a gun.

SELBY.   Not on every flight.

PASSENGER. I'll be ready. I'll kill myself rather than fall into their hands. I'm telling you so you won't get a shock when I keel over. There now, watch that one.

SELBY.   But it could be anyone. It could be me.

PASSENGER. Well I'm telling you, you won't pull a fast one on me because I have my cyanide capsule.

SELBY.   It isn't me.

PASSENGER. It could be you.

SELBY.   It couldn't be me because I work for a charity organisation and we don't get involved in any kind of political activity and that includes hi-jacking planes.

PASSENGER. You going to give out blankets and all that stuff?

SELBY.   I'm hoping to be the very first charity worker on the scene.

PASSENGER. Do you know the greatest tragedy of this hurricane?

SELBY.   Tell me and I'll see what I can do.

PASSENGER. Bananas.

SELBY.   Bananas?

PASSENGER. Do you know how much you guys at home are going to have to pay for bananas next winter?

SELBY.   How much?

PASSENGER. And do you know whose fault that is?

SELBY.   The hurricane?

PASSENGER. The peasants. The people you are coming to wrap up in blankets.

SELBY.   I'm sure they didn't mean to.

PASSENGER. They chopped down the trees. They chopped down the trees on the hillside. So when the wind and rain came pouring down there was nothing to hold the earth on the hills and smash glub yuk, there's mud ten feet deep over all the bananas in the valley.

SELBY.   Well I never did like bananas all that much.

PASSENGER. Wait, watch that one.

SELBY.   Why, what did he do? What? What?

PASSENGER. He acted normal.

SELBY.   What did they cut the trees down for?

PASSENGER. Because they're stupid, I guess. To grow food.

The landowners who arranged for us to have
the valley to grow bananas should have spelt it
out to the people: if you cut down the trees,
there's going to be soil erosion. But nobody told
them. They cut down the trees. Wallop.

SELBY.   It walloped them too. There's 8,000 dead.

PASSENGER. Yes, that's right, they brought all these tons of
rocks and mud down on their heads. If they
want to kill themselves, OK, but they don't have
to wreck the bananas.

SELBY.   Where did they used to grow food then? Before
they went up the hills and cut down the trees?

PASSENGER. Are you trying to get funny?

SELBY.   No, I just wondered where –

PASSENGER. You know perfectly well where they used to
live.

SELBY.   No I don't.

PASSENGER. In the valleys of course, where we grow the
bananas. Do you have any idea of the
importance of the export of bananas to the
business community of this country and to my
company?

SELBY.   No. Yes.

PASSENGER. Then you've some idea of the immensity of
this tragedy. I won't go into the figures. It puts
a strain on my heart. I'll just close my eyes and
meditate for twenty minutes.

SELBY.   Excuse me. Excuse me. Oh please, excuse me.

PASSENGER. It's not good for me to be interrupted when
I'm meditating.

SELBY.   I just wanted to get one thing clear.

PASSENGER. It makes me very irritable if I'm disturbed just
when I'm getting calm.

SELBY.   Are you saying the 8,000 deaths in this
hurricane were caused by the landowners and

the banana companies taking the valleys to grow bananas?

PASSENGER. Are you some kind of a communist? Are you going to hi-jack this airplane?

SELBY. No.

PASSENGER. Why don't you hi-jack this airplane and go to Cuba?

SELBY. Why don't you take your cyanide capsule?

PASSENGER. Stewardess!

SELBY. No, really, I just –

PASSENGER. Stewardess, I've caught a hi-jacker.

SELBY. No, really, there's been a misunderstanding.

56

SELBY. *She is backed up against bales of blankets she is handing out with one hand while trying to take photographs with the other.*

SELBY. Look I'm trying to take some photographs for our publicity, do you mind? Give the blanket back and I'll give it to you again, and this time I want you to smile, right? Smile? Smile? Does anyone here speak English? Cheese, cheese, formaggio. No, it's all right, you can have the blanket back, I just want –

57

SELBY *and a* GIRL. *Both are dirty and exhausted.*

SELBY. Was that three nights without sleep?

GIRL. I've lost count.

SELBY.	Well, I've finished. Every last bit of sticking plaster.
GIRL.	Yes, I've finished too.
SELBY.	Well.
GIRL.	Yeh.
SELBY.	And tomorrow start planning the long-term relief.
GIRL.	Don't talk about it.
SELBY.	At least there's no problem seeing what has to be done.
GIRL.	What has to be done?
SELBY.	Build the houses again. Put everything back like it was before.
GIRL.	You're planning to build another slum are you?
SELBY.	Let's think about it tomorrow.
GIRL.	Why do you think there's 8,000 dead?
SELBY.	The hurricane . . . and well the erosion, of course, the mud, the banana companies can't be left out of it. On the other hand they were very flimsy huts. Proper houses –
GIRL.	So there's 8,000 dead because of what it was like before?
SELBY.	Yes.
GIRL.	So you're going to spend your charity's share of the disaster relief fund putting everything back like it was before.
SELBY.	I thought you were tired.
GIRL.	I am.
SELBY.	Look, be realistic. Ninety per cent of the people here own 10 per cent of the land, right? You told me so yourself. And 3 per cent of the people own all the best land and grow bananas and sugar for export. Therefore, it's perfectly

obvious that anything we can do with the relief
money is bound to be leaving everything like it
was before unless the whole society changes. All
we can do is patch things up.

GIRL.   Some of the peasants have formed a league. The
landowners don't like it. Two men were shot
when they went to a union meeting.

SELBY.   Yes I know, it's very sad, but 8,000 –

GIRL.   There's talk of occupying some uncultivated
land and the peasants' league growing food
collectively.

SELBY.   There's always unrest after a disaster.

GIRL.   I'm going to recommend to my lot we use our
share of the disaster fund to support the
peasants' league.

SELBY.   I thought a hurricane would be . . . you
know . . . earthquakes, floods. Natural disasters.

GIRL.   A hurricane is just a strong wind. An
earthquake is just the earth moving. They're not
disasters till you get people.

SELBY.   I thought . . . you know . . . you can't blame
anyone. Act of God.

58

The MAYOR *and* SELBY.

MAYOR.   Act of God. Earthquake. Guatemala. Shockproof
houses, wealthy inhabitants, mostly all right.
Shacks on ravines, in Guatemala City alone
1,200 dead, 90,000 homeless. In the whole
country, 22,000 dead, mostly the poor –

SELBY.   All right.

MAYOR.   City official shot dead after suggesting homeless
          people should rebuild on unoccupied private
          land.

SELBY.   All right.

MAYOR.   Name a nonpolitical natural disaster.

SELBY.   Drought. Drought in the Sahel.

MAYOR.   Really?

SELBY.   Go on.

MAYOR.   Sahel. French colonial rule. Change in people's
          way of life. Cattle routes blocked, traditional
          rights to wells disregarded, crops they couldn't
          eat, overgrazing of pasture, people concentrated
          round a few wells instead of –

SELBY.   I get the idea.

MAYOR.   Act of God. No rain. Drought. Traditional ways
          of surviving drought gone. No reserves of food.
          Too many cattle for the pasture. Too many
          people in one area.

SELBY.   I said I get the idea.

MAYOR.   Famine.

SELBY.   Yes.

MAYOR.   All right?

SELBY.   An act of God is political, all right.

59

SELBY, *a* GUERRILLA *and a* JOURNALIST.

SELBY *is sitting under a tree.*
The GUERILLA *stands nearby with a gun.*
The JOURNALIST *approaches cautiously.*

SELBY.   Are you really there?

JOURNALIST. Yes.

SELBY.   Because sometimes I see things.

JOURNALIST. No, I'm a journalist.

SELBY.   Am I being rescued?

JOURNALIST. I'm being allowed a five-minute interview.

SELBY.   Take this message.

JOURNALIST. It's three months since you disappeared after sending a message back to your office that you wanted to learn more about the country before returning to London. It's been established that you then set off in a jeep. How soon were you captured by guerrillas?

SELBY.   The first day.

JOURNALIST. And could you tell me how that capture took place?

SELBY.   To Mr Dent, the director. And Mr Price.

JOURNALIST. And how are you being treated?

SELBY.   This is the message. Our share of the disaster emergency fund should be divided between the peasants' league and the liberation movement.

JOURNALIST. The guerrillas are demanding a ransom. That is the condition for your release? How much –

SELBY.   Their aim is to overthrow the government and introduce land reform.

JOURNALIST. How much are they demanding?

SELBY.   So tell Mr Price, the best way to help the people here is to help them with what they're doing, which is organise to fight oppression, and the quarter of a million pounds should all be given to help that struggle.

JOURNALIST. They are demanding a quarter of a million pounds ransom and have submitted you to a gruelling session of brainwashing.

SELBY.   Tell them I'm getting a bit bored sitting here under the tree. It gets very hot.

JOURNALIST. And how exactly were you captured?

60

PRICE *and some* BUSINESSMEN.

PRICE *is presiding over a businessmen's lunch. There are bananas on every plate.*

PRICE.   We've all made so much money importing bananas that I'm sure we'll be glad to give a little of it to charity, especially when we can have fun at the same time.

61

PRICE, DENT, SELBY, GUERRILLAS, PEASANTS *and* BUSINESSMEN.

A sideshow. The GUERRILLAS *and the* PEASANTS *stand at the back of a rifle-range being shot at by* BUSINESSMEN. *As they are wounded they crawl off and are replaced by others. Behind the stall,* PRICE, DENT *and* SELBY *are bandaging wounds and sending them back in.*

SELBY.   I'll have you patched up in no time and then you can go and be shot at again.

62

The MAYOR.

MAYOR. The royal python is another lovely snake, known
also as the ball python, no doubt from its habit
of curling up into a tight ball when alarmed.
You can roll it along the table just like a real
ball. But you can't force it to unwind, the more
you force it the more frightened it gets and the
tighter it stays rolled up. They like to eat live
food, of course, but you can feed them in
captivity on raw beef if you cover it with chicken
feathers or rabbit fur.

63

PRICE *and* SELBY.

SELBY *is in a hospital bed.* PRICE *is visiting.*

PRICE. It's lucky those soldiers rescued you when they
did because we'd already allocated the quarter of
a million, you know, for rebuilding houses and
for an old people's home and an orphanage for
a hundred children, so that we couldn't have
paid the ransom if we'd wanted to. And you
weren't even caught in the crossfire.

SELBY. I was very lucky.

PRICE. And you're feeling better, are you? Because
when you first arrived back in England you were
quite delirious. I'm sure you've forgotten the
things you said to me. And I've decided to
forget them too.

SELBY. I'm fine now, thank you.

PRICE.   You must have as long a holiday as you need,
          and let me know when you feel up to working
          again.

SELBY.   If it's all right with you, Mr Price, I think I'd
          like a break from the charity side of things.

PRICE.   It's what I like to see, Miss Selby, a young
          person spending a year or two working for
          charity and then coming back into the business.
          You've gained a great deal of experience and
          bring more to your work. You've certainly done
          your bit and it's high time you got on with your
          career. I'll be able to bring you in at
          management level.

64

SELBY *sitting behind a large desk.*

65

SELBY *and the* MAYOR.

SELBY.   Snake. Snakeskin. Handbags. Rich –

MAYOR.   Yes.

SELBY.   You must have seen that all along.

MAYOR.   Everyone has his little blind spot. I love my
          snakes. Relatively speaking, I would still go so
          far as to say a snake is not essentially political. A
          live snake is hardly political at all compared to
          anything you like to name. Name something.

66

SELBY *sitting behind a large desk.*

SEAGULLS

Characters

VALERY, middle-aged
DI, slightly younger
CLIFF, young, American

Green grass, clear sky.

VALERY *and* DI.

DI *looks at her watch.*

VALERY. I don't like it.

DI. What? What don't you like?

VALERY. Can we get tea?

DI. And cakes. I told them you'd like cakes.

VALERY. I don't like the open air.

DI. It's only for charity.

VALERY. I don't eat cakes before.

DI. You do.

VALERY. I don't any more.

DI. You still drink tea?

VALERY. What tea?

DI. You can eat the cakes after.

VALERY. Yes I can, you are lovely Di, I'm sorry I'm so nasty, I'm not in the mood today. I wish we were just here with nothing to do like everyone else. I wish I'd come to see somebody else do something wonderful instead of being the one.

DI. You enjoy it.

VALERY. You don't have to do anything.

DI *looks at her watch.*

DI. We've nothing on the whole of next week except packing and I'll do all that. We can go and watch other people every day. What would you like? We could go to a concert.

VALERY. You know I hate concerts.

DI.   What then? You don't in fact like watching other
           people do things.

VALERY.   Is there a circus on?

DI.   I can find out.

VALERY.   I'm like a performing elephant. Di, I really don't
           enjoy it any more. I'm like a chimpanzee on a
           bicycle.

DI.   If I was a chimpanzee I'd be thankful I could
           ride a bicycle and not be stuck in a cage all day.

VALERY.   I didn't mean you don't have to do anything.
           You're the one does all the work. I couldn't
           write letters and talk to people on the phone
           and make bookings. I wouldn't know how.

DI.   But you're the one it's all about. You're the one
           with the gift.

VALERY.   I think I'm a freak.

DI.   You know what you are. You're one of the first
           of a new species of person.

VALERY.   Well. It's bound to be tiring.

DI.   Of course it is. You're wonderful to keep going
           the way you do.

VALERY.   I.expect it's all right in the open air.

DI.   Nice to see the sun for once.

VALERY.   It smells nice. I never like the smell in
           laboratories. I don't expect I'll ever see daylight
           once I'm at Harvard.

DI.   And don't pretend you won't love it.

VALERY.   There's quite a lot of people.

DI.   Naturally.

VALERY.   And I'll just do it, and they'll all clap, and then
           it's done and we'll have tea and cakes. I'll have
           made all that money for – what?

DI.   There's a young man waiting. I said you
           probably wouldn't see him.

VALERY.   What sort of young man?

DI.   Nothing special.

VALERY.   No.

DI.   What I'm really looking forward to after you're finished with your scientists is the whole US tour. It's a dream to me. Chicago. Los Angeles. Little Rock Arkansas. New place every day. People cheering. You don't know who you'll meet. And next morning you just leave again.

VALERY.   Will people cheer?

DI.   Of course.

VALERY.   I suppose they will.

DI.   You wouldn't rather be working in Marks and Spencer's?

VALERY.   I might see that young man if you could find the tea.

DI *looks at her watch.*

DI.   Don't put yourself out.

DI *goes.*

CLIFF *enters.*

CLIFF.   Mrs Blair? It's very kind of you.

VALERY.   Not at all.

CLIFF.   I know how sick you must get of fans.

VALERY.   Not really.

CLIFF.   And just before appearing too. I thought you would probably have to rest.

VALERY.   No, I just have a cup of tea.

CLIFF.   I would have thought you'd have to prepare yourself. Like sit in solitude for a period of time and summon all your innermost energies.

VALERY.   Not all that much, no.

CLIFF.   You just go out there and do it? Mrs Blair, I
            have to say this, this is the greatest day of my
            life. That may sound foolish to you –

VALERY.   No.

CLIFF.   I've followed your career ever since I was a
            child. Before you got famous this last year or so
            I knew about you already because there was a
            newspaper story back in seventy-two about that
            time you were mad at your husband and objects
            such as frying pans and dishes started to fly
            through the air without you touching them. And
            you denied it, you know, but I thought this has
            got to be true. I pinned the cutting up by my
            bed. I was thirteen at the time and my dad was
            kind of a heavy drinker, well he still is, and I'll
            tell you, you and Flash Gordon were the two
            heroes of my childhood.

VALERY.   I don't know Flash Gordon.

CLIFF.   Mrs Blair, may I ask you something?

VALERY.   Please do.

CLIFF.   Why did you deny it? Why did you keep the
            world waiting five years?

VALERY.   I don't know really.

CLIFF.   My friends used to laugh at me.

VALERY.   I wasn't ready. I didn't mean it to happen.

CLIFF.   You didn't? You mean it just happened? I've
            wondered about that. What did you think just
            before it started happening?

VALERY.   You see, I don't remember.

CLIFF.   What was the last thing you said? Were you just
            so mad at him or what?

VALERY.   I don't remember.

CLIFF.   What had he done just before that to make you
            – I'm sorry. I do apologise. I have thought
            about this a great deal.

VALERY.   My little girls were only five and seven years old.

CLIFF.   I beg your pardon?

VALERY.   That's why I said I threw the frying pan with
           my hands. I didn't want to start – well, all this, I
           didn't know what it would start if I said I could
           move things.

CLIFF.   You denied it for the sake of your children?

VALERY.   I thought it would be more like other children
           for them if I said I'd just thrown the frying pan.

CLIFF.   That's terrible. Children don't like their mothers
           repressing themselves.

VALERY.   They were upset enough as it was.

CLIFF.   I have been a child myself quite recently.

VALERY.   But it wasn't that important to me. It was only
           that it got in the papers. I'd always moved
           things. When I was a child I thought everyone
           could do it.

CLIFF.   Did you really? I think that's beautiful.

VALERY.   Well it was stupid, wasn't it? I must have been
           very unobservant.

CLIFF.   And when did it dawn on you you were specially
           chosen?

VALERY.   I sort of forgot about it because it obviously
           wasn't something important like learning to read
           that your parents cared how you were getting on
           with it. I felt maybe it was like picking your nose
           or farting, everyone did it and pretended it
           didn't happen. So most of the time I forgot
           about it.

CLIFF.   Until one day – ?

VALERY.   No, it was just off and on, and in between I
           wouldn't think about it. I knew it wasn't normal.

CLIFF.   You must have felt very proud.

VALERY.   No, I didn't then.

CLIFF.　　You could hardly avoid it now.

VALERY.　　Well I do feel proud sometimes, I must admit. But then I get tired of it you know, I get bored with it.

CLIFF.　　You must get very upset when some people think it's all a fake.

VALERY.　　I'd think it was all a fake if someone else did it.

CLIFF.　　I think that's wonderful of you.

VALERY.　　I'm a very ordinary person.

CLIFF.　　No, Mrs Blair.

VALERY.　　Well I'm going to Harvard University in America next week for intensive investigations.

CLIFF.　　You know the US trains dolphins as a weapon of war. You want to be very careful.

VALERY.　　I only move quite small things quite small distances.

CLIFF.　　But potentially. You must feel that yourself.

VALERY.　　Well I do. I must admit.

CLIFF.　　It's the next thing after nuclear physics. Mind is the energy resource of the future.

VALERY.　　It's a funny feeling being so important.

CLIFF.　　Don't let them flatter you. It's how you use it.

VALERY.　　I don't usually like to say because it sounds silly or greedy but it does seem to me sometimes that the mind could really move mountains. I'm not saying my mind you understand, many many minds, if there were many minds that could do it, and maybe in the future, if it's true that I'm ahead of my time, if this is the way people are going to turn out or if everyone really can do it already —

CLIFF.　　Like you thought as a child.

VALERY.　　If they can and just haven't quite got the knack yet, then all those minds together could I don't know what. Send a rocket into space at least, I should think.

DI comes in with a tray of tea which she puts on the ground.
VALERY ignores her and the tea.
DI looks at her watch.

DI.   Don't exhaust yourself, dear, will you.

                DI goes.

CLIFF.   Was that a hint I should leave now?

VALERY.   Is that silly, do you think, a rocket into space?

CLIFF.   No, it's absolutely probable.

VALERY.   This afternoon I have to set off a firework. I just have to move a little knob and that sets off I don't know what but anyway it lights the fuse and off goes a rocket.

CLIFF.   I think that's a really great symbol of what lies ahead.

VALERY.   I do too. I sometimes think can this be me? I was working in Marks and Spencer's, you may know that –

CLIFF.   I do indeed, and how you caught the shoplifter. That's legendary, Mrs Blair.

VALERY.   I think deep down I must have decided it was time I did something.

CLIFF.   You had this secret power.

VALERY.   Everybody thought I was just an ordinary person and I'm not clever or pretty. If I had to say all I know about inflation or protecting the whale I'd be finished in thirty seconds. I've no skills, well I can run a home but you don't feel that's enough these days, my mother could just stay home and not worry but then she wasn't happy either. So there I was at Marks and the novelty of that had worn off, because at first it was a novelty just to go out to work again, I thought I can't go to work looking like this, I

felt shy. But of course you get used to it very
quickly, I wished it had been harder because I
was already bored and bored at home too
because it's very up and down and the girls are
getting on. Some days it seemed nobody had
spoken to me all day, well nobody had looked
me in the eye, just nothing at all had happened.
Things had happened of course but not so the
end of the day would be any different from the
beginning, and I'd had enough because of
course I knew what I could do. I think I chose
catching the shoplifter to get a big fuss, because
I said to Di, that's Di that's my manager now,
she was working there, that's how I knew her, I
said Di, look, and I didn't do it till she was
looking. Then I made the shirt he'd taken come
right back up out of the bag and on to the
counter. And that was it really and it's been non-
stop from that moment and my whole way
of life, you can imagine. But my daughters quite
like it because everyone at school says they've
seen me on television, and I'm not away all that
much. And I think my husband thinks more of
me than when I was nobody. And I do like it. I
like it when what I'm looking at starts to move,
and then everyone's amazed, and the professors
talk to you like someone who understands, and
you get to meet people and go places you never
would, and it's only sometimes lately like today I
haven't felt like doing it, and even sometimes I
find I can't do it. At home sometimes I think
shall I try, shall I do it, and it's like when you
can't remember a word or you can't swallow,
have you ever had that, sometimes for a split
second you can't swallow, my God, and then it's
all right, sometimes it's like that, I can't do it, I
think my God. And then either it's all right
again or else I just don't do it, I leave it, I do it
some other time, I leave it because it's no use
panicking. And I seem to get more tired now.
When I was a child I'd never feel any effect
from it but after a day in a science laboratory,
well it's harder work, my pulse rate goes up to

four times normal and my brain waves do
extraordinary things if you see afterwards where
they've recorded it, and I'm just exhausted for
hours sometimes, I lie there and I can't wake up
or go to sleep and I think one day I'm going to
die of this. But then next day I'm back again
because I suppose it has a fascination for me so
I keep trying, but when I was young I used to
do it so easily or even without knowing like the
time you read about when the frying pans and
dishes flew across the room and one of them did
in fact catch my husband on the ear, but of
course I pretended I threw them and everyone
thought he was crazy or drunk, which he was
anyway, but now of course all his friends –

She stops.

CLIFF.   What?

VALERY.   What?

CLIFF.   You were saying?

VALERY.   What?

CLIFF.   You were saying your husband's friends . . . ?
           Now appreciate how right he was and realise the
           truth of what an amazing woman you are.

VALERY.   Please go away.

CLIFF.   Mrs Blair?

VALERY.   I've talked a lot of nonsense.

CLIFF.   Believe me –

VALERY.   I'm tired.

CLIFF.   Yes of course, I'm sorry, you must rest and get
           yourself together for the great moment. I can't
           tell you how grateful I am for the opportunity –

VALERY.   Di! Di!

CLIFF.   Shall I find her for you?

           DI *enters.*

VALERY.   Di, I don't feel well.

DI.   What have you been saying to her?

CLIFF.   She's the one who's been doing the talking.

DI.   Off you go now, leave her alone.

CLIFF.   Goodbye, Mrs Blair. I hope you feel better. And believe me it's been a great honour. God, I never got her autograph. Do you think – no, sorry. Goodbye. Sorry.

CLIFF goes.

DI looks at her watch.

VALERY.   Di?

DI.   There now.

VALERY.   What the hell did you let me see him for?

DI.   You said you wanted to.

VALERY.   I hate talking.

DI.   I thought a fan would give you a bit of a lift.

VALERY.   It did at first but now I feel terrible.

DI.   You haven't drunk your tea.

VALERY.   I talked too much.

DI.   Just be quiet for a bit.

VALERY.   I talked such a lot of nonsense.

DI.   Here, drink this.

VALERY.   Mind you, he talked a lot of nonsense.

DI.   I'm sure he did. You shouldn't give your time to these people.

VALERY.   They don't understand and they will keep talking about it till it gets to be something quite different. I'm not seeing anybody afterwards. I'm never seeing anyone again.

DI.   You don't have to.

VALERY.   I hate talking about it, Di. I shouldn't talk about
          it. I should just do it. I don't like talking.

DI.   In ten minutes you are going to do it.

VALERY.   The tea's cold.

DI.   It would be by now.

VALERY.   It doesn't matter.

DI.   Hush now.

VALERY.   Di.

DI.   Yes, love.

VALERY.   It doesn't really matter.

DI.   What doesn't?

VALERY.   Talking.

DI.   Of course not, you deserve a bit of fun. Just you
          mustn't get tired out, that's all.

VALERY.   It doesn't matter because I'm going to do it in a
          minute, and that's all that matters, nothing else
          really. Hardly anything. Really nothing else
          matters to me Di except this.

          DI *looks at her watch.*
          The light brightens.
          *The machine is an elaborate mechanism inside a glass
          dome with a rocket attached at one side.*

          VALERY *stands by it, not moving.*

          DI *is standing well back and to one side.*

          VALERY *smiles. Then she is grave. She concentrates.
          This goes on.*
          Her face is red with effort.
          She half looks round at DI, DI *half steps forward, but*
          VALERY *turns back.* DI *stays where she is.*
          She goes on and on, motionless.

VALERY.   I think we'd all feel better if I stopped trying.

DI *and* VALERY. VALERY *is sitting on the ground. She puts aside a half-eaten cake.*

DI. My aunt's a remarkable woman. When her husband died she cried for a week and then for another week she didn't say a word, just sat staring at the wall. At the end of that time she went out and bought a wig and joined an amateur dramatic society. She was eighty-two. She went on holiday last summer to Italy. She said, 'The only thing I didn't like dear was all those old women sitting outside their houses dressed in black.' Don't you think we might go on holiday?

VALERY. I don't know.

DI. We could go for a week in Majorca.

VALERY. I want to go home.

DI. I'm seriously considering postponing Harvard.

VALERY. How can we?

DI. We can do what we like.

VALERY. They're busy men. They've got other work to do.

DI. They're not unique, Valery. You are.

VALERY. I don't want to go to Harvard.

DI. Two weeks in Majorca.

VALERY. I'd miss the children too much.

DI. We'll take the children. You can have two weeks in Majorca with your husband and children without me, if that's what you want.

VALERY. He couldn't take a holiday this time of year.

DI. You and the children then. You and me and the children.

VALERY. Do be quiet.

DI.   You're just exhausted, that's all.

VALERY. All the people. Were they given their money back?

DI.   If they ask for it. But they're not asking because it was for charity. And anyway they did see you, you did try, it's not as if they didn't see anything. People enjoy watching things go wrong.

VALERY. We can't afford a holiday, Di, because I won't be earning any more.

DI.   Of course you will.

VALERY. No, I'm finished.

DI.   You just need a rest.

VALERY. No.

DI.   You'll have a complete medical tomorrow.

VALERY. I'm not ill. I'm perfectly normal. I just can't do it any more.

DI.   Of course you can.

VALERY. No I can't.

DI.   All right, you're finished, it's over.

VALERY. Do you think so?

DI.   I don't know, do I? It could be.

VALERY. I'm just tired.

DI.   Maybe.

VALERY. I shouldn't have talked so much.

DI.   You think it was that?

VALERY. I've stayed up all night and still moved things. I lifted a table three feet into the air when I was drunk without spilling a glass.

DI.   Look Valery, don't start feeling sorry for yourself. If you think you're tired, then take a rest. Do whatever you need to get it working again and never mind the expense, it's an investment. This is our whole living at stake.

VALERY.   All right then. We'll take a holiday. Then we'll go to Harvard.

DI.   Postpone Harvard?

VALERY.   A week?

DI.   Two weeks.

VALERY.   What about the tour? What about all the bookings?

DI.   Look I'm the manager, will you leave me to manage? I'm not panicking. I'm not saying it can't be done. Just get well as fast as you fucking can.

VALERY.   I'm not ill.

DI.   Get working.

VALERY.   I'm going to, my God, I miss once and you start acting like this. You'd still be in the shirt department if I hadn't let you be my manager. You can't move objects with your mind. You don't understand anything at all about it. You're nothing. I can always get another manager.

DI.   If you can still do it, Valery, you can have ten managers tomorrow. On the other hand if you can't do it, there's nothing to manage, you're the one who's nothing. I've had considerable experience this year, I've got considerable contacts, I can always get other clients. I can start an agency.

VALERY.   Of course I can still do it. It's just because it was in the open air. I can't concentrate in the sunshine.

DI.   I always knew you wouldn't last but I thought you'd last longer than this.

VALERY.   You're fired.

DI.   You're not a job any more, there's nothing to be

fired from. You never really wanted to succeed.
You're frightened of it. You'd rather be sorry
for yourself, it's what you're used to. You don't
want to go to America, you're not up to it,
you're just little Mrs Blair that's all, you want to
go home to your family and make the tea, and a
few half-days in Marks and Spencer's. But I'm a
businesswoman. I'm on my way. And if you're
not going up any more I'll find someone who is,
because there's plenty of them.

VALERY. It wasn't about that. It was something I could do
in my mind and now I can't. Unless I still can.
I'll wait and see. I'll find out in the end.

DI. Valery. Why don't you just nudge that teacup
and see if it goes?

VALERY. No.

DI. Go on.

VALERY. I don't want to.

DI. If you can't it wouldn't make things any worse.
And if you can, then –

VALERY. I don't want to try.

DI. I'm sorry for what I said.

VALERY. Never mind. I expect I started it.

DI. I won't really leave you.

VALERY. I don't want you to.

DI. That's all right then.

VALERY. Well it's not, is it?

DI. Everyone's entitled to an off day.

VALERY. It's not the first time. It's been getting worse.

DI. It is the first time.

VALERY. It's the first time in public.

DI. You might have said. If I make bookings I'm
saying this is something good, I'm going to look
foolish.

VALERY.   So that's why I'm frightened.

DI.   I won't leave you.

VALERY.   Not yet you won't, just in case. But you will after.

DI.   You know something we could do. If you could just make it through Harvard so you've got your scientific guarantee, and then for the tour maybe we could find some way of working it.

VALERY.   Working it?

DI.   Fixing it. No, well, I didn't think you'd leap at that. Shall we go home?

VALERY.   Go away, will you?

DI.   I'll be in the car.

VALERY.   I'm getting a train.

DI.   Don't sulk, Valery.

VALERY.   I'll see you tomorrow.

DI.   Have you got enough money on you?

            DI *goes*.

            CLIFF *enters*.

CLIFF.   My first reaction was just to slink off. And then I thought, well everybody's just going to have slunk off and maybe you'd feel better if someone – anyway you only have to say and I'll . . .

VALERY.   It's very nice of you to bother.

CLIFF.   It's a kind of hard situation to know what to say in.

VALERY.   I'm sorry I let you down.

CLIFF.   No no, I'm sorry, I mean you must feel terrible. I know I feel terrible. But I've been thinking and you know what it is, it's just embarrassment. It was just appallingly embarrassing. Like when I was six I went to the bathroom in my pants in the museum and everyone was saying, What's this awful smell? So I joined in, I said, What's this awful smell? And then some of this shit ran down my leg and made this trail behind me on the floor of the museum, and one of the kids saw it and they all said, What's that? And I joined in, I said What's that guck on the floor? And they all knew it was me, and I knew they knew it was me, and I still said, What's that on the floor? That was my previous most embarrassing moment. But embarrassment's nothing really. You'll go on and do it fine and land rockets on the moon and your name will go down in all history books and statues to you in public places with pigeons on and people calling their babies Valery.

VALERY.   If I can't do it any more, I won't have this tour in America or anything. I won't have people coming round after to see me.

CLIFF.   You're still the person who did it before. You're still Flash Gordon.

VALERY.   Not if I can't do it.

CLIFF.   But if you did it before, even if you'd only done it once, there's bound to be other people. It's not a matter of you, it's a matter of human potential. I guess you're not too interested in human potential this afternoon.

VALERY.   I don't know if you still want my autograph.

CLIFF.   Of course, yes please. Really, I was going to ask you.

VALERY.   Best wishes to – ?

CLIFF.   Cliff.

VALERY.   Cliff. There. Thank you.

CLIFF.   Thank you. Look there's a story I thought about while I was watching you struggling away. I don't know if you can stand Chinese wisdom. There was this man and all the seagulls came

down round him and lit on his head and his
hands every time he went down on the beach.
And one day his father was very sick, and he
said to his son, Go down on the beach and get
me a seagull, I'm lying here in bed and I'd really
like to see a seagull. So his son goes down on the
beach and not one seagull comes near him. I
wonder if that's relevant at all.

VALERY.   I don't see what it has to do with the Chinese.

CLIFF.   I mean whether it's doing it for money, or doing
it when you're bored with it, or doing it in
laboratories, or doing it when you want to too
much, or whether it's just packed up like
somebody going blind. The fact that you can't
do it is in a way just as interesting as the fact
that you could do it. Somebody could do a
whole study about what causes these things not
to happen.

VALERY.   We don't know for certain I can't do it.

CLIFF.   Of course we don't.

VALERY.   You're talking about me as if I'm dead.

CLIFF.   I'm sorry.

VALERY.   You can't do it and you're still alive. Everybody I
see is walking around and they can't move heavy
objects with the power of their minds, and they
don't want to kill themselves because of that.
What keeps them going?

CLIFF.   Different things. I guess you've got used to
being extraordinary.

VALERY.   I sit here looking and there's the people and the
trees and the grass, and things are still moving.
Or not moving. It's just that I can't . . .

CLIFF.   There's plenty going on all right.

VALERY.   You can't do it either.

CLIFF.   I'll do something else. I haven't even finished
college yet. If you do get to the States I'll

certainly come to one of your showings. You
know I bet some people won't believe you
couldn't do it today. They'll think you pretended
to get everyone more interested. And people
who think it's all a fake anyway will think you
pretended to make it seem more real. I don't
really like to say this, but until today I kind of
always wondered if it was a fake. In fact, even
when I saw you couldn't do it, it just lurked in
the corner of my mind that it might be a really
great con trick. Even now I wouldn't bet my life
on it. I nearly would.

VALERY.   I loved it. It was all that mattered.

CLIFF.   That was another embarrassing moment.

VALERY.   It's rather cold.

CLIFF.   I love your English summers. I think they're
neat. You get these really unexpected skies.
What are you doing?

VALERY.   Nothing.

CLIFF.   I thought for a minute maybe . . . you know . . .
moving the teacup or something. No. Sorry.

VALERY.   No. No, I'm just watching.

CLIFF.   Watching what?

VALERY.   Watching things move.

THREE MORE
SLEEPLESS NIGHTS

Notes on layout

A speech usually follows the one immediately before it BUT:

1) When one character starts speaking before the other has finished, the point of interruption is marked /

e.g.
MARGARET. I don't dislike him / but that don't mean I
      fancy him.

FRANK. And he don't dislike you. Eh? Has he said that?
      He don't dislike you? He don't dislike you.

2) A character sometimes continues speaking right through another's speech:

e.g.
MARGARET. Your friend. I don't like him /

FRANK. You fancy him.

MARGARET. like that, I quite like him.

This applies even when the intervening speech is very long.

Characters

MARGARET
FRANK
PETE
DAWN

There are three scenes which happen in different rooms but
the set is the same all through, a double bed.

Three More Sleepless Nights was first staged at the Soho Poly, London on 9 June 1980. The cast was as follows:

MARGARET	Jan Chappell
FRANK	Fred Pearson
PETE	Kevin McNally
DAWN	Harriet Walter

Directed by Les Waters

MARGARET. Night after night you're round there, don't
bother lying, night after night, you can clear out
round and live there, I don't care. Night after
night / coming home pissed, what am I for,

FRANK. Shut it.

MARGARET. clean up your mess? Times I've cleaned your
sick off the floor, you was sick on the Christmas
presents Christmas Eve, time you shat yourself /
tell her that, she'd like that, clean up your shit.

FRANK. Shut it.

MARGARET. Give her something to think about. She thinks
the sun shines out of your arse, I could tell her
different, ten years / of you, let her try ten

FRANK. Shut up will you, five minutes peace, come
through my own front door you start rucking.
What sort of home's that? Any wonder I don't
come home, when I come in you start, any
wonder, Christ.

MARGARET. years, she don't know half, spruce yourself up
aftershave me mum give you Christmas, she
don't know who you are, thinks you walked out
the telly, that's what you fancy, someone don't
know nothing about you. You can come over
big, talk big, big spender, Mr Big, Mr Big Pig
coming home night after night / pissed out of
your mind, what mind you got to be pissed out
of?

FRANK. Shut up will you. I've not been there. I've not
been to see her two weeks now, not been round
there two weeks, I told you I was stopping
seeing her. She come up the garage dinner-time.
I says no, I told Margaret I'm not seeing you
and it's true I'm not seeing her, ask anyone,
ask Charlie. I been up the pub that's all.
/ I suppose I'm not let go up the pub now is

MARGARET. Ask Charlie.

FRANK. it, sorry mates my wife won't let me. I been up
the pub, I been to Charlie's for a few pints after,

ask Charlie / ask anyone, my wife's just checking

MARGARET. Charlie'd say anything.

FRANK.   up on me, she don't believe a word I say, don't
          believe a word I say, don't believe a word I say,
          do you? / What sort of marriage, what sort of

MARGARET. Ask her, shall I?

FRANK.   wife are you? What sort of marriage? What's
          left? What do I bother for? What I give her up
          for?

MARGARET. Go round there shall I, ask her, silly cow,
          she'd tell me too, all smiles, tears in her eyes,
          can't we be friends, can we fuck, must have been
          desperate to be friends with her anyone with a
          pram and a cup of tea, / can't think what

FRANK.   Might as well still see her, might as well go
          round there now. Your fault, you drive me, you
          drive me round there, don't believe a word,
          what's the point, you think I'm having it off,
          come in the door start rucking, might as well
          enjoy it.

MARGARET. you see in her, her hair's growing out too,
          looks dreadful, looks cheap, she's cheap, word
          my mum was fond of, cheap, see the point of it
          now, cheap. She don't look younger than me,
          she's five years, what you must think of me if
          you fancy that. Try to look after myself, / don't

FRANK.   I go round there now you know whose fault it
          is, what sort of marriage is this? What sort of
          wife are you? Come in my own front door.

MARGARET. look bad, could have been a model, could have
          been a hairdresser, could have been a shorthand
          typist easy the grades I had in Commerce, I had
          good speeds, could have been a temp made a
          fortune by now, secretary to an executive / gave
          it up to be a wife to you, could have took the pill

FRANK.   Yeah yeah yeah yeah yeah.

MARGARET. gone raving, could have had blokes wouldn't look at her, cheap she is, hair growing out, stupid cow, can't type even, can't read, what you must think of me if you fancy that. Puts you in your place, what you must be like, must be desperate, feeling your age a bit, take what's on offer, last chance, think what other blokes she's had / can't hold jobs, weirdos, that's where

FRANK. You fancy Charlie.

MARGARET. you're heading. Weirdos and winos, about it with her, all she can get. There was one looked like a goldfish couldn't shut his mouth come in handy I suppose with the kissing, surprised you can shut yours / all the time you spend round

FRANK. You fancy Charlie.

MARGARET. there, want to watch out you don't end up looking like a goldfish. I do not fancy Charlie /

FRANK. You like him don't you?

MARGARET. so don't start that. I quite like him. He's your friend. You're the one he tells

FRANK. We all know whose friend he is, you like him don't you?

MARGARET. lies for. Your friend. I don't like him / like

FRANK. You fancy him.

MARGARET. that, I quite like him.

FRANK. You quite like him, you quite like what you get, you quite like it, / you like it.

MARGARET. I don't get nothing.

FRANK. You don't get nothing. Not for want of trying. /

MARGARET. I don't try. I don't know what you're talking about

FRANK. Not for want of trying is it. No you don't try, too good aren't you, fancy yourself, he's not pulled that easy, you've no style, no class / he's got them queuing up, Charlie.

MARGARET. I don't want Charlie, I'm not interested, I love
you.

FRANK.   And you like him.

MARGARET. I don't dislike him / but that don't mean I
fancy him.

FRANK.   And he don't dislike you. Eh? Has he said that?
He don't dislike you? He don't / dislike you.

MARGARET. He's not said nothing.

FRANK.   That's a lie, never stops talking to you, / every

MARGARET. He's not said he dislikes me.

FRANK.   time I take you up the pub. I'm sure he hasn't
said he dislikes you / no, he wouldn't.

MARGARET. He hasn't said he likes me either.

FRANK.   Hasn't said he likes you? My heart bleeds. I'm
very sorry he hasn't said he likes you. You'll
have to make do with him touching you up. /

MARGARET. He don't.

FRANK.   You're wasting your time, seems to me. Don't
know why you don't get on with it / instead of

MARGARET. Nothing to get on with.

FRANK.   making me hang about. Nothing to get on with?
He thinks there is / oh yes he does.

MARGARET. How do you know what he thinks?

FRANK.   Oh it's only you knows what he thinks is it? /
What does he think? I should ask him, phone

MARGARET. I don't know what he thinks.

FRANK.   him up, ask him / go on, phone him

MARGARET. Don't be stupid.

FRANK.   up, ask him. He might say no he don't fancy
you, that would hurt your feelings / that would

MARGARET. No it wouldn't.

FRANK.   be a shock. Charlie not fancy you. I don't see
           why not, it would hurt my feelings if it was me,
           you ent got no feelings that's your trouble, think
           you're wonderful, don't care what nobody thinks
           of you. Just as well / way your skin's going

MARGARET. He's just a friend. He's your friend.

FRANK.   nobody's going to want to know. You're putting
           on weight too. You be friendly, I'm not
           bothered, you be friendly, you take him to the
           pictures, don't you stop for me. I'm not
           bothered. I'd move out if I was you, go on / why
           don't you move out leave me in peace, come in

MARGARET. I don't want to move out, I love you, why
           don't you listen to me, what you doing to us,
           what's it for?

FRANK.   my own front door start rucking. You want it
           both ways don't you, me and him, well I'm not
           playing that little game. Like him do you, I like
           him, bet he's got a big one eh? gets big for you
           eh? you'd like that wouldn't you? get all wet
           thinking of him eh? / think of him in bed

MARGARET. Night after night you come home pissed, I've
           had enough of you, serve you right if I did
           fancy Charlie, what if I did, what about you and
           her, round there every night, I know you are
           whatever you say.

FRANK.   do you? lying there thinking of him then give
           me a rucking, thinking of him were you? think
           of him when you're with me? pretend it's him
           do you? eh? Wasting your time there because
           Charlie wouldn't touch you if you was the last
           woman, he's said that to me, he's said that, only
           that time he was drunk last Christmas, you
           couldn't keep your hands off him at the party, I
           was ashamed to know where to look in front of
           my friends / if Charlie wasn't my mate

MARGARET. Where were you then, upstairs with her, that's
           where you were, Christmas party, who was sick
           on the presents?

FRANK   I'd break his neck, he knows that, he apologised
           to me, he didn't know what he was doing could
           have been his grandmother under the mistletoe
           if she come at him the way you did. I didn't
           know where to look, showing me up in front of
           my friends, at least what I do I do decent, I
           don't shame nobody, I take her different places
           than what I take you / don't go the same pub,

MARGARET. Take her with a different prick do you?

FRANK.   nothing, nobody knows, I don't flirt like you do,
           it's all right between me and her, it's not flirting,
           it's something special you wouldn't understand, /

MARGARET. All right is it?

FRANK.   I go in her door don't get this /don't get

MARGARET. I don't understand, I don't want to
           understand.

FRANK.   rucking, get some peace after a day's work talk,
           about cheap, you're cheap / anyone

MARGARET. Piss off round there then and I hope it's
           something special and I hope you get a hot
           dinner with it and your socks washed –

CHILD   (*off*). Mummy.

FRANK.   you can rub up against at a party, nobody's
           interested are they that's the trouble, you don't
           want me, that's what it is, you don't want me,
           you'd have anyone else you could get, you don't
           want me, you can't get nobody else /

CHILD   (*off*). Mummy.

FRANK.   that's all it is / You don't want me.

MARGARET. Shut up, shush, wait.

           Silence.

FRANK.   Go on then go and see him, don't mind me,
           everyone's more important than me / just has to

MARGARET. He'll go off, sh.

FRANK.   call out, drop everything.

        Silence.

MARGARET. I don't want a row. / Put out the light.

FRANK.   I don't want a row. I want a good night's sleep before tomorrow. Set the clock have you? /

MARGARET. 'Course I've set the clock.

FRANK.   Didn't go off this morning.

MARGARET. That was yesterday. It went off all right this morning /you didn't wake up, that's all.

FRANK.   Whichever day it was. Set it properly have you?

        FRANK *puts out the light.*

        You don't enjoy it with me, you don't want me that's what it is, you don't / enjoy it with me, you

MARGARET. Oh God.

FRANK.   said that I remember every word you say, you said that, don't deny it, you said it, / can't

MARGARET. I said it once, I said I didn't enjoy it that time, I didn't say I don't enjoy it.

FRANK.   get out of it now. No man wants a woman don't want him, stands to reason, only human, Christ, you think I'm a fucking machine, you got a washing machine, drying machine, fucking machine / I'm not your fucking fucking machine.

MARGARET. Didn't enjoy it that time my God you was drunk, you just been with her, you said she was better than me, she moved about more, what am I supposed to do? I'd had a day and a half with the kids, Johnny had tonsillitis / you never come

FRANK.   You're talking about a year ago.

MARGARET. home till late, you said you'd be in, I'd cooked spaghetti and you never come home, Johnny wouldn't stay in bed till I hit him, not move about, I'm surprised I was conscious, move

about more, hell, what does she do, do it in a
track suit does she? / go jogging, do it while
she's jogging?

FRANK.   Look, I don't think she's better than you, why
am I still with you? I think you're the greatest,
that's why I stopped seeing her, you're better
than she is / I stopped, I give her up, you don't
believe me what's the point, I might as well go
and see her again, I'll go tomorrow night, don't
expect me home because I won't be home
tomorrow night.

MARGARET. I'm not going in for this competition,
I don't care who's winning your little prize
because I'm not going in for it. I don't have
to compete because I'm your wife, you're
already mine, I won already, some prize /
I'm not competing. Why

FRANK *puts the light on.*

FRANK.   Is there anything to drink?

MARGARET. should I have to pull my stomach in for you, is
my hair all right, you're who I live with, I'm not
going in for it, I'm not putting make-up on in
bed. / If she's what you want, if that's

FRANK.   I've had a hard day.

MARGARET. the sort of person you are, my mistake I ever
married you. You've always had a hard day. /
You think I don't have a hard day? Lift wasn't

FRANK.   Yes I always have a hard day and who's it for?
Come back to this any wonder I don't come
home? Who has the money off me eh? Who has
the money?

MARGARET. working again for three hours, I put off going
to the shops then I had to go or they'd have
shut, there was no bread left, I carried the
whole lot up the stairs and the bag broke / the
eggs fell out, there's no eggs for breakfast you

FRANK.   It's your job. I don't moan, I get on with it,

what's wrong with this country nothing but moans, country of old women.

MARGARET. can do without, 32p the eggs, you've had your eggs in beer, you've had your kid's dinners and your kid's new shoes and your kid's school journey he can't go on because that would be a luxury / he don't need it like you need six pints.

FRANK. Who earns it? Who earns it? Sooner I'm dead, then you'll see who earns the money, see what's what, see what it's like / managing on your own.

MARGARET. Get a job myself, get a job up the school, school helper, could get that now / think I will,

FRANK. What you get for that? Nothing.

MARGARET. you can't support your family by yourself / better go out to work and help myself, enough of your talk.

FRANK. Don't tell me I don't support my family, don't you say that. If my dad heard you say that, what he'd do if my mum said that, don't you say I don't support my family. Who has the money off me? If you can't make it last that's your lookout, you buy the wrong stuff / you buy

MARGARET. You give her money.

FRANK. frozen food, my mum never let us go hungry, you're no good in the house, rotten housekeeper, you buy rubbish. If I give her money, if I lend her money it's my money to lend. She's a woman on her own bringing up a child, I'd expect to hear more human sympathy from you / always on about feelings, you got no feelings for other people, only got feelings for yourself.

MARGARET. Not enough money for the school journey he could have gone to the sea and you give her money, your own kid, showing him up in front of his mates, your own kid and you give the money to her, give her the whole lot I should, give her the housekeeping and let her cook our dinner / frozen food, you'll be lucky if she can

FRANK.   You got no feelings, I don't want to talk to you.
           I don't want to listen. I don't like you.

MARGARET. see out past her eyelashes to cook a fishfinger.

           Silence.

FRANK.   I'm not very happy. Are you happy?

MARGARET. No.

FRANK.   My fault, is it?

MARGARET. I'm not saying it's your fault / but . . .

FRANK.   But.

MARGARET. Come on, I don't want a row.

FRANK.   Who's starting a row?

MARGARET. I can't even talk to you without you shouting
           at me because /

FRANK.   Who's shouting?

MARGARET. you're too pissed to have /

FRANK.   Who's pissed?

MARGARET. a proper talk.

FRANK.   Eh, who's pissed?

MARGARET. I'm not for one, I don't get to go out / it's you
           goes out.

FRANK.   You want a drink? Do I stop you having a
           drink? You can buy drink in the supermarket, is
           it my fault you don't enjoy yourself / you make
           yourself a martyr, if I take you down the pub

MARGARET. Drink at home by myself, no thank you, old
           lady with a gin bottle.

FRANK.   you don't enjoy it or you start chatting up
           Charlie don't you, think I'm stupid, blame me
           for everything, go on blame me, that's what I'm
           for / come home at night so you've someone to
           moan at.

MARGARET. I do have feelings, you wouldn't know, you're
never here, you don't know nothing about me,
night after night round with her or up the pub
or out with Charlie, wherever you are it's not
here, that's all I know, what am I doing sitting
here waiting for you night after night, never
here when you're needed like the time I had the
miscarriage where were you? you knew I'd
started and you went to the pub and you went
to Charlie's / you're here for the fun but that's

FRANK. Didn't know what was happening, did I?

MARGARET. all, here for the beer, you did know what was
happening, you're a liar, you always was a liar,
you stopped out on purpose / you knew, you did

FRANK. This is five years ago, do us a favour, this is five
years ago.

MARGARET. know, could have died all you cared, I don't
care if it's ten years ago I'll never forgive you /
and every time you go out now I'm not

FRANK. You don't want me. You don't want me.

MARGARET. surprised, I think yeh yeh, that's him, off he
goes, selfish bugger / what do you expect what

FRANK. If I could afford it, I'd leave you. If I could get
a place.

MARGARET. are you surprised for, haven't you learnt yet
that's what he's like, think he loves you stupid /
course he don't. Why don't you go

FRANK. If it wasn't for the money and the kids.

MARGARET. and live with her, she's got a nice place. Don't
stay with me just to keep yourself in beer, go
and live with her, / see how you like it.

FRANK. Don't want to live with her. I don't even like
her, don't know why I keep seeing her. I was
round there tonight / is it any wonder? First

MARGARET. I knew you was.

FRANK. time for a week, / I don't know.

MARGARET. I'd like to put a brick through her window. I'd
              like to round with a gun and she opens

FRANK.   Stop talking stupid.

MARGARET. the door and I shoot her in the stomach. If it
              wasn't for the kids I'd get a gun. I'd like to see
              her bleed. I'd like to stamp

FRANK.   Shut it. Shut it.

MARGARET. on her face. She's not that pretty. /What

FRANK.   It's not her.

MARGARET. you must think of me.

FRANK.   It's not you.

2

PETE *and* DAWN *are lying on the bed.*
A long silence.
PETE *asks* DAWN *if she's all right:*

PETE.   Uyuh?

DAWN.   Mmm.

PETE.   Ah.

DAWN.   (*moans*). Ohhhhh.

            A short silence.
            PETE *asks how* DAWN *is:*

PETE.   Mm?
            Mmm?

DAWN.   Uh.

            A long silence.
            PETE *puts out the light. He asks if it was all right to*
            put out the light:

PETE.   Uh?

Silence.

DAWN.   Ohhhhh.

Silence.
PETE *is comfortable:*

PETE.   Ah.

A long silence.
DAWN *wakes with a start:*

DAWN.   Oh.

PETE.   Huh?

DAWN.   Ohhhhh.

PETE.   Mmmm?

A long silence.
DAWN *moans,* PETE *acknowledges.*
DAWN *is fed up with the night,* PETE *sees where
things have got to:*

DAWN.   Ohhhhh.

PETE.   Mmm.

DAWN.   Ugh.

PETE.   Uh huh.

A short silence.

The plot of *Alien* is very simple. You have a
group of people and something nasty and one
by one the nasty picks them off. If you're not
going to see it I'll tell you the story. Mm?

DAWN.   Mm.

PETE.   There's these people in a spaceship, right, and
it's not like *Startrek* because the women wear
dungarees and do proper work and there's a
black guy and they talk about their wages. So
they get a signal there's something alive out in
space and it's one of their rules they have to
investigate anything that might be alive, so
they go to see what it is, right, and a couple of them
go poking about on this planet and it's like a

weird giant fossil and they find some kind of eggs, and go poking about, and then there's a horrible jump and this thing gets on to John Hurt's face. They let him back in the ship and this horrible thing's all over his face and how can they get it off, that's quite unpleasant. Then it gets off itself and disappears and he gets better. And then there's the horrible bit everyone knows about where he's eating his dinner and it comes bursting out of his stomach and there's blood everywhere and it looks like a prick with teeth, a real little monster, but it's worse in the stills than in the movie because it goes so fast you hardly ever see it. That's quite good, I like that, when you think they might have shown it you all the time and they don't.

DAWN *puts the light on;* PETE *protests:*

Errr.

DAWN.   I feel completely unreal.

Silence.
DAWN *gets up.*

PETE.   Uh?

Silence.

I like movies where nothing much happens. Long movies, you can just sit there and look at them. *The Tree of Wooden Clogs* is a long movie. I wished they didn't have an interval.

A long silence.

DAWN.   I don't know if I'm unreal or everything else, but something is.

PETE.   Uh huh.

Silence.
PETE *gets a book and reads.*
DAWN *dials a number on the phone. There's no reply.*

DAWN.   I think I'm dead.

Silence.

PETE.   We could have something to eat.

Silence.
PETE goes on reading.
He asks if she wants something to eat:

PETE.   Mm?

DAWN.   Mm.

PETE goes out.
DAWN gets dressed, beautifully, in a dress.
She sits on the bed.
PETE comes back with tray of food including a loaf
and a knife.

PETE.   Ooh?

DAWN.   I thought I might go out.

PETE.   It is three in the morning.

DAWN.   Ah.

PETE.   Don't let me stop you.

DAWN.   Right.

PETE eats.
DAWN doesn't eat much.

PETE.   Then there's this creature you see loose in the
        spaceship and it might take any shape and it
        might get any one of them any time, and of
        course it does. There's a lot of creeping about in
        the dark looking for it and wondering when it's
        going to pounce and what it's going to look like.
        If you're looking forward to being frightened
        you can be frightened but a friend of mine went
        to sleep because it was so dark.

Silence.
PETE eats.
DAWN gets undressed.
PETE asks if she wants any more food; she says no.
He is pleased to eat it:

Uh?

DAWN.   Uhuh.

PETE.   Mmm.

             Silence.

DAWN.   I'm frightened.

             Silence.

PETE.   You'd think from those German movies that
             Germans were always sitting about not doing too
             much and staring into space and then whenever
             you meet Germans they're not like that at all,
             they're very adult. I suppose the movies seem
             quite different there.

             Silence.

             I'm thinking of *The Left-handed Woman. The
             Goalkeeper's Fear of the Penalty. The American
             Friend.* No, there's more rushing about in *The
             American Friend.* I won't tell you the plot, it's
             quite confusing.

             Silence.

DAWN.   I'm frightened.

             Silence.
             PETE *finishes eating.*

PETE.   The most frightening bit of *Alien* for me was
             when one of the crew turns out to be a robot
             and his head comes off.

             Silence.
             PETE *asks* DAWN *if she's all right:*

PETE.   Uyuh?

             PETE *puts some music on and goes to bed.*
             DAWN *phones again, again no reply.*

PETE.   I haven't seen my brother for two years.
             I haven't seen my mother for five years.
             I haven't seen my father for ten years.

             Silence. Music.

             Redupers, that's another German movie. It's short

for the all-round reduced personality. Did I see
it with you?

Silence. Music.
DAWN plays with the knife.

DAWN. There's a voice in my head, no there's not a
voice in my head, come on. *I keep saying to
myself in my head, I want to be dead, I want to
be dead,* and I don't think it's true.

Silence. Music.

PETE. So eventually there's no one left except this girl
and she runs away up and down the spaceship a
whole lot of times. And she gets away in a little
escape space ship and thinks she's safe and of
course the thing's in there with her. And she's
getting undressed, which I thought was a bit
unnecessary but I suppose it makes her more
vulnerable is the idea, and in the end she gets
the door open and it's sucked out into space. So
she gets a good night's sleep which is more than
I can say for some people.

DAWN takes the knife and gets into bed.
PETE is getting sleepy. He's glad she has come to bed.
*He asks if she's all right. She says yes. He settles down
more comfortably:*

Mmmm. Mmm?

DAWN. Mm.

PETE. Ahhhhh.

Long silence. Music.
They are lying back to back.
Under the sheet DAWN cuts her wrist.
PETE stirs:

DAWN. Ah –

PETE. Uh?

Silence.
Blood begins to come through the sheet.
The music ends.
PETE reaches out and puts out the light without seeing.

3

MARGARET *and* PETE.

MARGARET. I was so insecure that was part of it.

PETE.   You had no life of your own.

MARGARET. I was just his wife, I wasn't a person.

PETE.   You can't blame him though I mean.

MARGARET. I don't. I don't any more. I'm sorry for him.

PETE.   Yes, I'm sorry for him.

MARGARET. He's still drinking. He hasn't changed.

PETE.   You're the one who's changed.

MARGARET. I've changed. I was just his wife before. I had
            no life.

PETE.   You can't blame him. It's what you learn to be
            like.

MARGARET. It's what you learn but you can change
            yourself. I've changed myself.

PETE.   I'm not saying a man can't change.

MARGARET. You've changed, you say you've changed.

PETE.   I have yes but I can see, as a man, what the
            problem is for him.

MARGARET. You're not like a man in some ways not like
            what I think of a man when I think what's
            wrong with men.

PETE.   I'm still a man. I've just changed.

MARGARET. We've both changed.

PETE.   Yes.

MARGARET. It was getting the job made the difference. If
            I'd met you before I got the job I'd have got in
            a panic, I'd have thought is he going to marry

me or what, is he going to be a father to my
children, I couldn't just be happy. When I
decided to go for being a nursery assistant and
get some training, that was amazing for me to
think I could get trained and do something.

PETE. You can't, though, can you?

MARGARET. No, I can't but that's the cuts.

PETE. At least you know what you want to do.

MARGARET. That's it, I've got some idea of myself. I used
not to be a person.

PETE. I think you're wonderful.

MARGARET. When I saw him last week it was like seeing a
ghost. It's better when the kids go round to him
and I don't see him. It makes me feel like a
ghost myself. It used to be so horrible, you can
feel it in the air when you meet. I don't want to
be like that any more. You wouldn't have liked
me.

PETE. I would, I would have known.

MARGARET. I was horrible.

PETE. You were very insecure.

MARGARET. I had no life of my own. I was just his wife.

PETE. I was horrible. I could hardly speak. I couldn't
talk to Dawn. You and I just lie here and talk
but I'd got with Dawn so I didn't know what to
say to her. And she couldn't talk. It was me
killing her. If we'd stayed together she'd be dead
by now, she'd have done it in the end so it
worked, she'd be dead. I was doing that.

MARGARET. She was putting a lot of pressure on you.

PETE. She was asking for help.

MARGARET. You couldn't put the world right for her.

PETE. I could have talked. I was out of touch with my
feelings.

MARGARET. You're not now.

PETE.　　No, I'm different now and she's different. If I run into her now she's fine, chats away, we chat away perfectly all right. I didn't want her depending on me like that, I couldn't put the world right for her, I couldn't take the pressure. I hated London, I hated what it was doing to the kids I taught, I could hardly walk down the street let alone sort her out, I couldn't take it.

MARGARET. You needed someone less dependent.

PETE.　　It was a very destructive relationship.

MARGARET. You were out of touch with your feelings.

PETE.　　I dream about her with that sheet covered in blood.

MARGARET. We talk about them a lot.

PETE.　　Of course we do.

MARGARET. We say the same things over and over.

PETE.　　I suppose we're bound to for a bit.

MARGARET. Of course we are.

PETE.　　We have learnt.

Silence.

MARGARET. If I can't get the nursery training I'll have to do something.

PETE.　　Of course you will.

MARGARET. You say of course I will but it's not that easy, I can't even be a helper now they've cut the helpers. I don't want to be at home all the time, I'm a bit frightened of that. And I need money.

PETE.　　You don't have to make a martyr of yourself with the housework.

MARGARET. I don't make a martyr.

PETE.　　No.

MARGARET. It just makes sense if I'm the one who's here

and you're at work.

PETE.   I can't help it. I cook.

MARGARET. Of course you do and the kids are mine, the mess is mine.

PETE.   Don't worry so much about money. I'm earning money.

MARGARET. That's your money.

PETE.   I want to go to sleep.

MARGARET. Are you unhappy?

PETE.   I'm tired.

PETE *puts the light out. Silence.*

The microchip can do a billion thought processes in a second.

MARGARET. You can't get a speck of dust on it.

PETE.   When I'm out of work too I'll clean the floor.

MARGARET. You can do it Saturday.

Silence.

When did you last see Dawn?

PETE.   Last week sometime.

MARGARET. Which day?

PETE.   Wednesday, Tuesday.

MARGARET. Where was it?

PETE.   She was in the pub dinner-time.

MARGARET. Don't you have to be at school at dinner-time?

PETE.   No.

MARGARET. I thought you did special football dinner-play.

Silence.

PETE.   You see Frank more than I see Dawn.

MARGARET. I don't see Frank.

Silence.

MARGARET. Everyone's going to have to have hobbies.

PETE.   Everyone's going to be on the dole.

MARGARET. It's the future, you have to go forward.

PETE.   Who's going to make money out of it?

MARGARET. Think of robots. Don't you like the thought of robots?

PETE.   You're very wide awake.

MARGARET. Sorry.

PETE.   Sorry but I do have to get up in the morning.

A long silence.

I'm very wide awake now.

MARGARET. Uh?

PETE.   Sorry.

MARGARET. What?

PETE.   Sh.

MARGARET. Mm.

Silence.

Are you asleep?

PETE.   No.

MARGARET. What's the matter?

PETE.   I'm worrying.

MARGARET. What about?

PETE.   Fascists.

MARGARET. What?

Silence.

Is it us?

PETE.   What?

MARGARET. You keep being unhappy.

PETE. What makes you think it's us?

MARGARET. You used to be happy.

PETE. I'm happy about us.

MARGARET. Then what's the matter?

    Silence.

    What is it?

PETE. I don't know.

MARGARET. What sort of thing?

    Silence.

    It's not surprising I think it's us. If you keep being unhappy and won't tell me. I can't help thinking when I'm on my own. I know I'll be better when I get a job. I don't like being on my own and I know your meetings are important but I get frightened in the evening when the kids are asleep, I think what have I done? You don't like me talking like this, I can't help it, I've no one else to talk to, sometimes I don't talk to anyone all day, I can't help it if I'm frightened.

PETE. I'm going to put the light on.

    PETE *puts the light on.*

MARGARET. I don't want to say this but I worry about Dawn. You keep seeing her, you say you run into her, what you keep running into her for? If you're seeing her why not say so, I don't mind, I'm just afraid you might go back to her. I don't mind nothing if you tell me, it's when you don't tell me I think you're hiding something, I think you're seeing her and not telling me, is that true? I don't like lies, I never did like lies, I know I'm insecure and why shouldn't you see her, sleep with her if you want to, you're perfectly free, we're not married, I don't want to be married, never again, I don't want me and Frank, I wasn't a person, and you and Dawn, I

don't want that, so what are you doing? Night
after night out at meetings, I know they're
important, I get frightened, what have I done, I
left him for you, what have I done to the kids,
what's happening, and are you always at a
meeting or do you see Dawn, is that stupid? I
want to make you happy and I can't and I get
frightened and you've got to tell me everything.
I don't want to be like this, you've got to help
me, please say something.

A long silence.

PETE.   I don't know what to say.

MARGARET. No.

PETE.   I'm not doing this deliberately. I've stopped
being like this.

MARGARET. Yes.

PETE.   Are you definitely not going to see *Apocalypse
Now*?

MARGARET. I don't like war films.

PETE.   There's this guy who's already a war veteran and
he's back in Vietnam, he's a wreck but he can't
keep away from it, and he's given a mission to
go up the river and find this colonel who's gone
mad and kill him, right.

MARGARET. Right.

PETE.   So he goes on a boat up the river to find him.
And the main thing is these amazing set pieces
of destruction, it starts with a sort of still grey
shot of the jungle and it bursts into flames and
the whole thing looks stunning, planes coming
over and things exploding, and there's music. So
he's going up the river on this boat to find the
mad colonel and kill him, or maybe not kill him,
he's sort of attracted by him and we are, of
course, because we know it's Marlon Brando.
And on the way the Americans are killing
everybody and there's a mad officer who gets his

soldiers to go surfing and on the boat they kill a girl and rescue a puppy and the black kid on the boat gets killed and it's a real nightmare and he goes on up the river to find the colonel.

HOT FUDGE

Notes on layout

A speech usually follows the one immediately before it BUT:

1) When one character starts speaking before the other has finished, the point of interruption is marked /

e.g.
COLIN.   Nobody, / they went to Greece.

RUBY.   Nobody unless people who'd say I've been to Turkey.

2) A character sometimes continues speaking right through another's speech:

e.g.
JUNE.   They're explaining it. And not too fast. / You

MATT.   I go to a building society.

JUNE.   all right, Ruby? Don't mind him. Yes, I'm listening.

3) Sometimes a speech follows on from a speech earlier than the one immediately before it, and continuity is marked*

e.g.
GRACE.   You must feel like you're the nerve centre.*

HUGH.   We'll soon be able to drive anywhere in France within twelve hours but I could still offer you a watermill with conversion potential of fifteen bedrooms for just under eighty-five thousand.

RUBY.   If someone acquired it as a hotel you could put me in touch –

HUGH.   And you could arrange the holidays.

COLIN.   *It is exciting / making connections.

Characters

RUBY, about 40
COLIN, about 40
JUNE, Ruby's sister, slightly older
CHARLIE, her husband
SONIA, their daughter
MATT, her boyfriend
JERRY, a global manager, American, 20s
GRACE, a tennis teacher, Jerry's wife, American
HUGH, an estate agent, 40s
LENA, Colin's ex-wife.

The play takes place one evening:
    Pub: 7 p.m.
    Winebar: 9 p.m.
    Club: 11 p.m.
    Colin's Flat: 1 a.m.

Hot Fudge was given a performance reading at the Royal Court Theatre Upstairs on 11, 12, 15, 19, 22 and 26 May 1989. The cast was as follows:

RUBY	Gillian Hanna
COLIN	Allan Corduner
JUNE LENA	Carole Hayman
CHARLIE HUGH	Philip Jackson
SONIA GRACE	Saskia Reeves
MATT JERRY	David Thewlis

Pub: 7 p.m.

MATT, SONIA, CHARLIE, JUNE *and* RUBY.

MATT.   I wear a suit.

SONIA.   He does / look more . . .

CHARLIE.   You can wear pink satin. That's not the point.

MATT.   Yes, because they have to believe.

SONIA.   He looks completely . . . / You'd be surprised.

CHARLIE.   Look sweetheart we're not talking about would *you* be impressed / if he asked you out to dinner,

JUNE.   You don't listen, Charlie. He don't listen.

CHARLIE.   if he asked for your hand in marriage in his suit I daresay if I was a prospective father-in-law I daresay yes we would all be impressed by Matt in a striped shirt and a suit, that is not the point.

JUNE.   Tell us the point then, Charlie.

CHARLIE.   She's always like this on the third vodka. Two she likes me, four she's all over me, but she always has a go / on the –

JUNE.   I hope he's nothing like him.

CHARLIE.   Who's not? You hope / who's –

JUNE.   Nothing, my big mouth.

CHARLIE.   Who's not like me?

JUNE.   Ruby's giving me such a look now, / I don't dare.

CHARLIE.   What are you up to, Ruby?

JUNE.   No, leave her alone.

CHARLIE.   Who's the lucky man / this time?

SONIA.   We're trying to explain something.

JUNE.   If your father would listen.

CHARLIE.   What I don't like is it's messy. You don't just go in one bank, out, you're done. You keep going in and out all different banks, / every time you

SONIA.   Building societies.

CHARLIE.   go in you're giving them another chance to get you.

SONIA.   Every time you go in you're making money.

JUNE.   Explain it then because / I don't really . . .

CHARLIE.   I like cash in my hand.

SONIA.   You / get cash.

JUNE.   They're explaining it. And not too fast. / You all

MATT.   I go to a building society.

JUNE.   right, Ruby? Don't mind him. Yes, I'm listening.

MATT.   I go to a building society. This is the simple version. I go to a building society / and open an

JUNE.   In your suit.

MATT.   account, yes in my suit, and open an account in a false name. Sonia goes to a different building society and she does the same.

CHARLIE.   Identification.

MATT.   Does nicely.

CHARLIE.   So that sets you back?

MATT.   Say two hundred but that's a clean one because I know a postman and you can use it / for going out or –

SONIA.   Or one of those one-year travel documents is good.

CHARLIE.   And what do you put in to open the account?

MATT.   Say ten.

CHARLIE.   Ten's enough?

MATT.   Ten's fine but you can put in twenty, you can put in a grand, whatever makes you feel good doing it.

JUNE.   And this is what you've been doing, you've already / done this?

SONIA.   Yes, we've done it, we're / doing, wait

JUNE.   I hope you know what you're . . .

SONIA.   a minute / till we –

MATT.   So I've got the account and I've got the chequebook. And I write a cheque to Sonia though of course not Sonia but whatever she's called herself and she pays it into her account.

CHARLIE. And it bounces.

SONIA.   No, because, I said, it's a building society. A bank clears a cheque in three days, right, but a building society takes five.

MATT.   But they don't publicise / the fact.

SONIA.   But they can't keep you hanging about five days or the punters'd all piss off to the high-street banks like normal. So their little green screen says I've got five thousand.

JUNE.   So you cash it.

SONIA.   No, you don't want cash –

CHARLIE. I want cash.

SONIA.   You don't want cash yet because if you take it straight out they wonder. In fact, you can, I have done that but / only –

MATT.   But only if you've got plenty / of –

SONIA.   Only if you've got several cheques in so it looks as if there's plenty, say ten, and you take two out and let the rest go. / But I'm talking about the

JUNE.   Let the rest go?

SONIA.   basic way you do it and you don't / want cash –

MATT.   You're not exactly short of cash when you do this.

SONIA.   You do it say fifty times, you have to multiply.

CHARLIE.   Who wants another drink?

But he doesn't move and no one pays attention.

MATT.   So what she does.

SONIA.   So what I do is I get a building society cheque /
            right, because –

MATT.   Because the Skipton can't bounce.

SONIA.   A building society cheque for four thousand –

MATT.   Because it looks better if you don't take the lot.

SONIA.   Payable to Matt in another name.

JUNE.   Is that the same other name he had before?

SONIA.   No, it's better if it's another other name, / or
            Ruby or –

MATT.   So meanwhile I've another account and I pay in
            this very impressive building society cheque,
            which can't bounce. And *then* I take out maybe
            three thousand in cash maybe even the next day
            / and pay it –

SONIA.   Because they're impressed by a building society
            cheque.

MATT.   And I take the three thousand and pay it into
            another account. And that's a real solid three
            thousand.

            Pause.

CHARLIE.   When I was your age I just went in. I'm not
            saying it didn't take planning. But you did it.
            And somebody might get hurt, you hoped not
            but somebody might, that could be one of them
            or one of you. You had to take more with you
            than a suit.

MATT.   What are you saying? I don't shoot people? No,
            I don't shoot people.

CHARLIE.   I never shoot – don't start that with me.

MATT.   What's the matter with it?

CHARLIE.   Don't start.

MATT.   What's the matter with it?

CHARLIE.   I don't like plastic.

JUNE.   But we could do it. It's not so difficult we couldn't do it.

CHARLIE.   I'm not saying it's difficult.

MATT.   He's saying it's soft.

SONIA.   You can still go to prison just as much.

CHARLIE.   And that's another thing. What are you getting my daughter involved in? At what point / do they check up –

MATT.   It was her idea.

CHARLIE.   Then I don't expect it works.

MATT.   It does work.

SONIA.   Why don't we just forget it?

           Pause.

RUBY.   You have to be quite brave.

JUNE.   Ruby does it.

RUBY.   You have to be quite brave to lie so much.

           Pause.

CHARLIE.   The point is I have *done* time, I have already, I'm not looking for . . . In, out, you know where you are, if it was interesting I'm not saying I wouldn't be interested. But it's going to be constant aggravation. I would lose sleep.

JUNE.   It's true you don't sleep well. He don't sleep well as it is.

SONIA.   We've plenty of friends we can ask.

           Pause.

JUNE.   Ruby lies all the time, you do Ruby, you can

walk into places and talk. But I've never done credit cards. We're used to cars and jewellery and *not* talking. I can have a suitcase full of God knows what under the bed and I'm not bothered, I don't have to handle bank managers. That would be the difference.

Pause.

MATT.   If you don't sleep well as it is, you've nothing to lose.

JUNE.   I sleep. I sleep all right now. But once I've got all those names / and dates.

SONIA.   No, I'll keep track, you'd only have to go in. It would be better with more people because I've got fifteen accounts already. I go right out to the end of the tube lines. And now I've got one in Basingstoke and one in Brighton and yesterday I went to Derby.

JUNE.   I'm going to do it, I don't care.

SONIA.   I can't show my face in a Woolwich in London now. The more of us there are / the harder for

JUNE.   You're a clever girl. Isn't she a clever girl, Ruby?

SONIA.   them to work it out.

MATT.   And the harder for us.

SONIA.   No, Matt's brilliant, he's got a chart.

CHARLIE.   Who wants a drink?

He establishes that they all do and goes.

MATT.   Good.

JUNE.   He'll come round.

MATT.   I'm not bothered.

Pause.

JUNE.   So what's he like?

RUBY.   I like him.

JUNE.   What's he do?

RUBY.   He's got his own company.

JUNE.   Doing what?

RUBY.   Media monitoring. / I don't know. He's

SONIA.   Media what? Telly?

RUBY.   successful.

JUNE.   So how far's it got?

RUBY.   Not now.

            Pause.

SONIA.   So tomorrow shall we come over home and work
            some things out?

JUNE.   Come in the morning. Can you come in the
            morning, Ruby?

RUBY.   Tomorrow morning?

JUNE.   When are you seeing him?

            CHARLIE *comes back with drinks.*

CHARLIE.   Suppose we do it.

MATT.   OK.

JUNE.   You're wonderful, Charlie. He's wonderful.

CHARLIE.   Fourth vodka.

JUNE.   I go into the Woolwich and open an account
            with ten pounds. And I write Ruby a cheque for
            five thousand and she pays it into the Abbey
            National. Then she takes out / a building

MATT.   We've got three people working on IDs.

JUNE.   society cheque for four thousand payable to
            Sonia. Then Sonia takes out three thousand
            cash.

CHARLIE.   Does everything split five ways?

MATT.   It depends how much we each do.

CHARLIE.   We must talk about it.

MATT.   We will talk about it.

SONIA.   We're meeting tomorrow morning.

CHARLIE.   No, I'm collecting a car in the morning.

RUBY.   Before you talk about five ways. I'm wondering if I might want to stop.

JUNE.   But we want to do it with you.

RUBY.   But I might want to stop.

MATT.   What's the matter?

RUBY.   I don't mean pull out and let you down. If I stop opening any new ones.

SONIA.   But you're good at it.

RUBY.   Yes I know.

MATT.   Don't you want to be earning money?

Pause.

SONIA.   Are you frightened?

RUBY.   No.

Pause.

JUNE.   It's her new young man.

CHARLIE.   What is going on? / Who is this?

SONIA.   You haven't told him?

RUBY.   He thinks I run my own travel agency.

They laugh.

CHARLIE.   So who is this?

JUNE.   She only just met him.

CHARLIE.   Then what's he got to do with it?

RUBY.   I only said I might.

JUNE.   You don't want to wind it down unless you're getting married.

SONIA.   Or not even then.

MATT.   So shall we still count you in?

            Pause.

CHARLIE.   I lose sleep anyway over the cars. When I took
            the Lamborghini to Dieppe I didn't sleep the
            night before or two nights after.

JUNE.   And you was seasick. / He was seasick.

CHARLIE.   And I was seasick.

            They laugh.

Winebar: 9 p.m.

RUBY *and* COLIN.

COLIN.   Turkey, Turkey has risen astronomically.

RUBY.   It has.

COLIN.   Five, ten years ago who went to Turkey?

RUBY.   Nobody.

COLIN.   Nobody, / they went to Greece.

RUBY.   Nobody unless people who'd say I've been to
            Turkey.

COLIN.   Yes, people / who'd –

RUBY.   People who were discovering / would go to
            Turkey,

COLIN.   Yes, like India.

RUBY.   who were looking for adventure / and no loos.

COLIN.   Like India when we were young, people would
            go overland to India, but that means / going
            through –

RUBY.   But anyway you can fly to India, plenty of

people go to India for two weeks.

COLIN.   I know someone who went to India for the weekend.

RUBY.   The weekend?

COLIN.   A long weekend.

They laugh.

RUBY.   But of course the news from Turkey –

COLIN.   Politically it's very dodgy.

RUBY.   So you could help me with the latest –

COLIN.   Do you want a complete rundown on Turkey? Or salmonella? Or *perestroika?*

RUBY.   So everything's / at your fingertips.

COLIN.   Or the ozone layer? Or signal failure? Or Iran?

RUBY.   I don't do holidays in Iran.

They laugh.

COLIN.   But there must still be undiscovered . . .

RUBY.   There are of course but the development / is –

COLIN.   Even in Spain if you go inland.

RUBY.   Of course if you know where to look.

COLIN.   Which I'm sure you do.

RUBY.   And then there's Thailand.

COLIN.   I have been to Thailand.

RUBY.   When was that?

COLIN.   A long time ago, about seven years, / with my

RUBY.   It's changed a great deal of course.

COLIN.   ex-wife in fact. Holidays were one of our strong points.

RUBY.   Some people quarrel on holidays.

COLIN.   No, we had brilliant holidays, in fact. Our

problem was we both worked too hard, she's a
quite remarkable woman, / a top designer, not

RUBY. Do you keep in touch?

COLIN. cut out for marriage, oh yes, we're the best of
friends, / one has to be adult, life's too short.

RUBY. That's wonderful.

COLIN. What I did want to do was to go to China.

RUBY. It's still possible to go to China.

COLIN. Provided I take my bullet-proof vest.

RUBY. People go to China for two weeks.

COLIN. For the weekend?

RUBY. No, maybe not for the weekend.

They laugh.

COLIN. So it's holidays of character. Not package.

RUBY. Not package holidays but individually tailored
holidays. You can stay in a villa and then go in a
Rangerover.

COLIN. So it's adventure –

RUBY. It's luxury adventure. It's pick'n'mix.

COLIN. Like a week here . . .

RUBY. And a week on a camel.

COLIN. Or skiing.

RUBY. Skiing / and then scuba diving or –

COLIN. Windsurfing. Hangliding. Parachute jumps?

RUBY. Dolphins.

COLIN. Dolphins?

RUBY. People like to see dolphins.

COLIN. I've eaten dolphin.

RUBY. Eaten?

COLIN.   I'm sorry, I have.

RUBY.   That's all right, I'm not a / vegetarian.

COLIN.   But people talk to dolphins.

RUBY.   They talk to plants, would you eat a plant?

COLIN.   Yes I would, I particularly like spinach. I don't talk to spinach.

They laugh.

COLIN.   You're lucky in your chosen field because everything in the world is a potential commodity. Every lake, every town, every donkey walking by. Every single person in the world is either a potential customer or a potential commodity in so far as they are part of the ambiance.

RUBY.   You could say the same about your / field.

COLIN.   Yes you could, every bit of news / is –

RUBY.   Everything that happens / in the world –

COLIN.   Everything newsworthy –

RUBY.   Everything newsworthy that happens in the world is a commodity for you.

COLIN.   So the point of the existence of everything in the world is us.

They laugh.

Club: 11 p.m.

RUBY, COLIN, JERRY, GRACE *and* HUGH.

JERRY.   I feel that a career in global industry offers a lifetime package as exciting as it is possible to conceive.

COLIN.   You need flexibility.

GRACE.   You need interpersonal skills.

HUGH.   The world is certainly getting smaller.

GRACE.   And you must find that, Colin, with all the world news pouring into your / office.

COLIN.   Yes, I'm certainly very aware of the village / aspect.

GRACE.   You must feel like you're the nerve centre.*

HUGH.   We'll soon be able to drive anywhere in France within twelve hours but I could still offer you a watermill with conversion potential of fifteen bedrooms for just under eighty-five thousand.

RUBY.   If someone acquired it as a hotel you could put me in touch –

HUGH.   And you could arrange the holidays.

COLIN.   *It is exciting / making connections.

GRACE.   And exhausting.

COLIN.   It is, it's a constant / high.

GRACE.   Connections are so significant.

JERRY.   Colin will appreciate the importance for the international manager of giving weight to local tastes, cultures and traditions.

COLIN.   Yes, you have to forge a bond / with people on the ground.

GRACE.   You have to relate to elementary differences / in outlook.

JERRY.   And the company that cannot do that will be humbled.

COLIN.   So if you need background information / on

JERRY.   Yes, I'd certainly appreciate . . .

GRACE.   And you must face the same issue, Ruby. You

COLIN.   your growth areas. The recent upheavals in Yugoslavia.

RUBY.   Yugoslavia.

GRACE.   go to research the vacations yourself?

RUBY.   And I do make great friends / with the local people.

GRACE.   Because they are individuals.

HUGH.   If you can spare the time, we're operating three executive aircraft making regular weekend viewing trips to Brittany / and Normandy.

RUBY.   I don't think I'd want to tie myself to a house.

COLIN.   Ruby's / more of a gypsy.

HUGH.   You should look on a home as an investment.

JERRY.   Personally I prefer property to the markets. Currency shifts are a random walk. I'm hoping to eventually buy an island.

HUGH.   It's a bit late to pick up bargains in the north but if you went as far as the Pyrenees you'd soon benefit from the ripple effect.

GRACE.   Do you offer tennis vacations, Ruby? I ask because tennis is my subject.

RUBY.   Tennis courts are available / on a great many –

GRACE.   I don't need a court. What I do is teach tennis off-court. / I could teach by the pool. There is

RUBY.   Off-court?

GRACE.   no ball, you visualise the ball. And more important you visualise yourself. You visualise yourself hitting the ball. Group therapy eliminates mental blocks thus freeing the body, Alexander eliminates physical blocks thus freeing the mind. But the important thing is to convince yourself and others that you are a winner. Are you into self-development vacations?

RUBY.   Stress vacations, / the hot springs at Bled in

GRACE.   Wonderful.

RUBY.   Yugoslavia / are recommended for all

COLIN.   No riots at Bled.

RUBY.   managerial diseases. / No, exactly.

JERRY.   The global management stress / factor . . .

HUGH.   Anyone who can afford one house can afford
            two, anyone who can afford one house *needs* two
            to get away / from the stress of –

JERRY.   Because no large-scale business can afford to
            take other than a global view. And the local
            community has to recognise that. And that can
            be a source of considerable stress. It's a sad fact
            of life, Colin, that most realities have no regard
            for national boundaries.

GRACE.   So would you be able to accommodate the
            tennis?

RUBY.   I'd love to hear more about it.

GRACE.   Let's do lunch.

COLIN.   If you want to get away, you need a Lynx
            Eventer, which is a Jaguar stripped down and
            rebuilt as an estate car. There are only forty of
            these in the entire world. It would certainly give
            you boy racer credibility.

GRACE.   He is a boy racer, / that's exactly –

COLIN.   Or one of the exact replicas of the fifties D type.

HUGH.   With the tail fins.

COLIN.   You couldn't tell it from the real thing without a
            magnifying glass and the real thing would be
            half a million.

GRACE.   I do think genuine classic style . . .

HUGH.   New houses the same, classic style. You can buy
            Elizabethan style with a galleried hall.

JERRY.   We're talking image like with a company image.
            / It's very important just now

GRACE.   You have a great image.

JERRY.	to green our image.
COLIN.	You need an update on the current state of greening in multinationals.
JERRY.	It's the key marketing challenge / of the nineties.
COLIN.	Your biggest problem with image / is agrochemicals.
GRACE.	Pollution is certainly / a
JERRY.	We also have a problem with products that have
GRACE.	major story.
RUBY.	Beaches.
JERRY.	carrying fluid in the coating process.
HUGH.	There's a development near Cadiz where you can have an individual antique door tastefully incorporated. Just that one thing completely changes the image.
RUBY.	You have to think of the positive –
HUGH.	You have to act positive, there was a property by the sea no one could shift because of a sewage works, so they built a bypass and lined it with flowering shrubs / and shifted the whole lot.
JERRY.	It's a situation where we do go local rather than international in that if we accepted the optimum safety standards we couldn't compete in certain countries with local business. So we comply with the minimum legal requirement in that particular country.
COLIN.	I don't think you have an alternative, / Jerry.
JERRY.	An ecological wash may *be* clean but does it look clean? It is optical bleach that spells *clean* in this world, it is dazzling whiteness.
COLIN.	So where can we go where the beaches aren't full of shit?
GRACE.	Yes, Ruby, could you design a vacation for us? Jerry is in great need of a rest. / If I called in to

JERRY.   I can't get away right now.

GRACE.   see you tomorrow could we work something
            out? I don't have the address / of your agency.

RUBY.   I wish I could but we're completely run off our
            feet with company clients and / can't take
            individual –

COLIN.   Ruby's too exclusive / for us.

GRACE.   Ruby, that's too bad, I didn't realise. So where
            would you recommend for our vacation? We're
            not talking Europe / are we if we're talking

RUBY.   Gambia.

GRACE.   clean. And Colin will have to monitor world
            news / to make sure it's

RUBY.   Hugh can find us a house.

HUGH.   Bit far afield for me.

GRACE.   not a trouble spot.

JERRY.   We may well find ourselves in a / trouble spot.

HUGH.   Turkey. I can do Turkey. There's no Turkish
            tax / on gapital gains

COLIN.   And we'll go there in the Lynx Eventer.

HUGH.   provided you hang / on for two years.

JERRY.   That's one of the challenges of global
            management.

Colin's Flat: 1 a.m.

RUBY *and* COLIN.

RUBY.   So there I am in the speedboat which has no
            speed at all, in fact it's going back / wards
            because of the tide and the wind towards the

COLIN.   Backwards.

RUBY.   rocks, we're being swept out, so either we'll hit
           the rocks or we'll miss them and be swept right
           out round the head / land which is worse

COLIN.   Headland.

RUBY.   because then we'll be out at sea and nothing
           between us and the coast of Af / rica, and one of

COLIN.   Africa.

RUBY.   the women starts screaming —

COLIN.   You're not screaming.

RUBY.   I'm not screaming aloud because I have to
           pretend everything's under control and I'll have
           them back at their villa in no time.

COLIN.   But inwardly you're / screaming.

RUBY.   Inwardly I'm hysterical.

COLIN.   So there you are being swept out.

RUBY.   Nearer and nearer the rocks.

COLIN.   Not the open sea.

RUBY.   By then I would have welcomed the open sea.

COLIN.   And you hit the rocks.

RUBY.   No we didn't hit the rocks because in the nick of
           time I saw another boat crossing the bay and it
           was / Pedro —

COLIN.   Pedro.

RUBY.   Pedro from the village / who'd —

COLIN.   Who'd warned you.

RUBY.   Who'd warned me in the first place about hiring
           boats from Carlos and I'd dismissed it because I
           thought it was all part / of the vendetta over the

COLIN.   Part of the vendetta.

RUBY.   olive grove, and I was almost too proud to shout
           for help but —

COLIN. But there were the rocks.

The phone rings.

RUBY. There were the rocks so –

Pause.

COLIN. The machine's on.

The phone stops ringing.

There were the rocks.

RUBY. So I shouted and everyone shouted and we thought he hadn't heard us –

COLIN. He was probably serving you right.

RUBY. He probably was, and we could see the spray and the boat wasn't just going backwards, it was starting to turn, it was caught in a / whirlpool –

COLIN. Eddy, a whirlpool, my God.

RUBY. when he turned towards us and threw a rope, and it missed, and then he threw it / again and that was it, he towed us back to the harbour.

The phone rings.

COLIN. I'm glad you weren't smashed up on the rocks.

RUBY. Hadn't you better answer?

COLIN. I have a machine.

Pause.
The phone stops ringing.

I feel as if I've known you for years.

RUBY. Is it three weeks?

COLIN. Two and a half.

RUBY. Yes, I feel that too.

COLIN. I think we're very alike.

RUBY. In what way?

COLIN. We really go for things. We enjoy life. / We

RUBY.   Yes, that's true.

COLIN.   believe in ourselves. We like ourselves so we're
          able to like each other.

RUBY.   And we do.

COLIN.   We do very much.

          Pause.
          The phone rings.

RUBY.   It may be an emergency.

COLIN.   You're an emergency.

RUBY.   But really hadn't you better?

COLIN.   What emergency? My parents are dead already.
          I don't like my brother.

RUBY.   You don't have children?

COLIN.   I would have told you by now if I had children.
          Do you have children?

RUBY.   No, no I don't, but when the phone keeps
          ringing –

COLIN.   It's probably some nut.

          The phone stops.
          Silence.
          They kiss.
          Silence.
          The phone rings.
          COLIN *answers the phone.*

COLIN.   For fuck's sake.
          Just wait till the machine . . .
          The machine was on, you could –
          No, not now.
          I said don't.
          What if I do?
          Why don't I call you tomorrow and –

          The other person has hung up. COLIN *hangs up.*

          That was my ex-wife. Did I mention her?

RUBY.   You said you'd been married.

COLIN.   Yes, I have been.

RUBY.   Recently?

COLIN.   Off and on.

RUBY.   So is something the matter?

COLIN.   No no, it's fine.

RUBY.   Nobody's ill?

COLIN.   No no, everybody's fine.

Pause.

She's coming round. I told her not to but she will.

RUBY.   Do you want me to go?

COLIN.   I want her to go.

RUBY.   Is she unhappy?

Pause.

RUBY.   We'll be nice to her.

COLIN.   Yes, we will.

RUBY.   Because after all we're happy.

COLIN.   You make me very happy.

RUBY.   Good.

COLIN.   She'll be here in a minute.

RUBY.   Where was she phoning from?

COLIN.   The box on the corner.

RUBY.   Why didn't she come straight here?

COLIN.   We don't like seeing each other.

RUBY.   Then why –?

COLIN.   Because I didn't answer the phone and she saw the light.

RUBY.   Why was she phoning from the call-box?

COLIN.   What?

RUBY.	Does she live nearby?
COLIN.	No.
RUBY.	Then why – never mind.
COLIN.	She goes for walks at night and ends up at the call-box.

Pause.

She won't stay long.

Pause.

She has a key. She'll just walk in.

Pause.

RUBY.	Maybe I'll go home, it's very late.
COLIN.	I hoped you were staying.
RUBY.	Yes, but –

LENA *comes in.*

LENA.	I haven't forgotten the night you locked /
COLIN.	Ruby, this is Lena.
RUBY.	How do you do.
COLIN.	Lena, this is Ruby.
LENA.	me out of the house, I should have known then. Have you ever been locked out of the house, Ruby? You have that treat in store. Why did you have the machine on? You knew / I'd ring.
COLIN.	I don't have the machine specifically / to annoy
LENA.	Please speak for as long as you like after the tone beeeeeeeep.
COLIN.	you funnily enough. I have the machine for my friends and business contacts / who
LENA.	Business.
COLIN.	might ring up while I'm out.
LENA.	How's business?

COLIN. Do you want something particular because this isn't a good time.

LENA.   I thought you were getting an office.

COLIN. I have an office.

LENA.   Then why do they ring here? They ring here because the office is in the bedroom. Have you seen the office?

COLIN. Lena, we'll talk / tomorrow.

LENA.   It's a very small / office.

COLIN. We'll talk tomorrow.

LENA.   This is where he throws me out, like the time he locked me out of the house. What was I meant to do, I was banging on the door, I was / shouting –

COLIN. You were drunk.

LENA.   *I* was drunk, that would explain it, you never had a drink ha ha, and you couldn't be in the room with somebody / drunk –

COLIN. You'd been with the yellow toad. / She'd been with –

LENA.   Which shows what a bad time you'd been giving me, it was only you running round after teenage girls / or I'd never have looked –

COLIN. She was twenty.

LENA.   And the little ginger one, or wouldn't she have you? Wanted a proper man I should think, / not

RUBY.   I'm going home.

LENA.   a pervert who can't do it without imagining you're hanging upside down over a slow fire and he's the rescuer or is he the torturer, / first one then the other –

COLIN. She's crazy. Don't go. She's crazy.

LENA.   Who's crazy? Who's been in the bin, you or me?

Who's the one with the nervous breakdown, raving bonkers more like it, jealous maniac, have you found that? Having me followed, opening my letters, / taking my pants to a private

COLIN.   And what did I find? Wasn't I right? Weren't you a bitch?

LENA.   detective, and mean with it, never a penny to spend without where's it gone, I had a piss sorry I'm so extravagant with your hard-earned cash ha ha, lived off me more than I lived off him, complete wreck, unemployable now, self-employed he calls it, self-unemployable, sitting all day banging his head on the wall –

COLIN hits LENA and she falls down.

COLIN.   Cunt. Fuck you. Cunt. Fucking break your fucking get out of fucking cunt I'll –

LENA gets up. She hits COLIN and he falls down. He gets up.

RUBY.   I thought you'd hurt her.

COLIN.   She's used to it.

Pause.

None of that's true you know. She's a pathological liar.

Silence.

I could make some tea.

But he doesn't move.
Silence.

RUBY.   Is your office in the bedroom?

COLIN.   Yes, it is as a matter of fact. Why?

Silence.

The girl was twenty.

Silence.

RUBY.   What was that about a breakdown?

Silence.

You know the speedboat?

COLIN. Yes.

RUBY. That never happened.

COLIN. Ah.

RUBY. I haven't got a travel agency at all.

Pause.

COLIN. Right.

Silence.

RUBY. I didn't think you'd hit her.

COLIN. Well.

Silence.

Every morning I get two copies of every newspaper so I can cut everything out. I video all the newses and newsnights and . . . I hadn't worked for a long time and I am beginning to get customers.

Pause.

I hate the news.

Pause.

I sit in the bedroom all day and drink lager and stick video-tapes in the recorder.

Pause.

RUBY. I don't like your friends.

COLIN. No, I don't like them either.

RUBY. Haven't you got any nicer ones?

COLIN. They're the successful ones.

RUBY. Are they the only ones?

COLIN. I have got some others but I thought you'd like those ones.

RUBY.   No.

           Pause.

COLIN.   So is everything you told me about yourself a
           lie?

RUBY.   Just about.

COLIN.   Why is that?

           Pause.

COLIN.   So there's quite a lot to find out.

RUBY.   Yes.

           Silence.

           So what was that about a breakdown?

           Silence.

           Blackout.